IMAGES
of America

ROUTE 66
IN CHICAGO

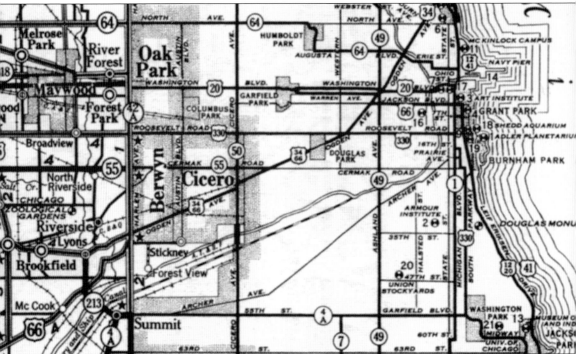

This detail from the *Official Road Map of Chicago and Vicinity*, printed on the reverse of the *Official Map of Illinois Highways 1935*, shows Route 66 entering the Chicago area from the southwest (lower left). Coming through the villages of McCook, Lyons, and Stickney, Route 66 joins Ogden Avenue in the city of Berwyn and then follows Ogden Avenue through the town of Cicero into Chicago. The route turns east onto Jackson Boulevard and terminates at Michigan Boulevard.

On the cover: Lou Mitchell's Restaurant and Bakery has been serving great food since 1923. Mitchell was 14 years old when his father, William, started the eatery, originally located across the street from its present location at 565 West Jackson Boulevard. The Mitchell family was ready to serve when Union Station opened for passenger rail travelers one block east in 1924, and when Jackson Boulevard became a state highway and then U.S. Route 66 in 1926. The restaurant has become the traditional place to eat before starting a journey west on "the highway that's the best." (Author's collection.)

IMAGES
of America

ROUTE 66
IN CHICAGO

David G. Clark

ARCADIA
PUBLISHING

Published by Arcadia Publishing
Charleston SC, Chicago IL, Portsmouth NH, San Francisco CA

Printed in the United States of America

Library of Congress Catalog Card Number: 2007924199

For all general information contact Arcadia Publishing at:
Telephone 843-853-2070
Fax 843-853-0044
E-mail sales@arcadiapublishing.com
For customer service and orders:
Toll-Free 1-888-313-2665

Visit us on the Internet at www.arcadiapublishing.com

This book is dedicated to Homer R. Clark of Joliet and to
Dorothy J. Michal of Chicago. They married in 1948 and started me on
the highway of life in 1957. They taught me that if one takes the time
to look out the window while traveling down the road,
chances are one will find something worth seeing.

CONTENTS

ACKNOWLEDGMENTS

My writing career began in 2002, when the National Historic Route 66 Federation accepted my first article concerning Chicago and the mother road for the *Federation News*. Thanks to David and Mary Lou Knudson for getting me started.

Thanks also to Bob Moore and Paul and Sandi Taylor of *Route 66 Magazine* for their support of my articles and first book, *Exploring Route 66 in Chicagoland*. Thanks also to Kathleen Miller and Jim Jones, editors of the Route 66 Association of Illinois' 66 *News*, for their continuing support.

Jim Conkle and the other staff members of the *Route 66 Pulse* newspaper have always provided support as has Pres. John Miller and the other officers and members of the Route 66 Association of Illinois. Thanks also are due to Patty Kuhn and Patty Ambrose of the Illinois Route 66 Heritage Project and Kaisa Barthuli and Michael Taylor of the National Park Service Route 66 Corridor Preservation Program.

Many of the writers of articles, books, and Web sites with a Route 66 theme have provided inspiration through their work. Notable among them are Marian Clark, Swa Frantzen, Carl Johnson, Jerry McClanahan, Russell Olsen, Scott Piotrowski, Jim Powell, Jim Ross, Tom Teague, Michael Wallis, and John Weiss.

I relied heavily on the work of people who have researched Chicago's history, including David M. Young, William Cronon, Frank A. Randall, John D. Randall, and the editors of the *AIA Guide to Chicago*, the *Encyclopedia of Chicago*, and *Chicago's Famous Buildings*. The *Chicago Tribune* from 1869 to 2001 was also very important.

The images in this book are mainly from my own collection. However the images from the Krambles-Peterson archive, courtesy of Art Peterson, provide an irreplaceable glimpse at the shared history of transit and highway. Also in the book are images from the Historic American Buildings Survey and Federal Office of War Information, courtesy of the Library of Congress.

I also thank Melissa Basilone, my editor at Arcadia Publishing. Her guidance made the process of completing this book enjoyable.

Finally this project would have been impossible without the sacrifice and encouragement of my partner in life, Carol Krohn. Thanks again for everything, my dear!

INTRODUCTION

My father was born in Joliet, and my mother was from Chicago. They married in 1948 and moved to Hammond, Indiana. A triangle of highways connected my childhood home and those of my parents; a trip to my maternal grandmother's home in Chicago required a drive north along U.S. Route 41, and the Clark family farm near Joliet was due west on U.S. Route 6. The hypotenuse of that triangle, connecting Joliet with Chicago, was Route 66.

Starting in the early 1960s, my family explored America by car each summer with month-long vacations. One year, we planned a tour of the state parks of Illinois. After visiting a historic site north of Springfield, we realized we had time to venture further from home than originally anticipated. We noted that St. Louis was only 100 miles away, so we decided to visit the Gateway Arch. Our Illinois trip suddenly included a drive further southwest along Route 66.

Although Route 66 traversed eight states, its usefulness for our family was for travel of a much more local variety. The highway's nickname as the "Main Street of America" was apropos, since it served travelers whose destinations were across town as well as across the continent.

In 1933–1934, Chicago hosted the *Century of Progress*, a world's fair highlighting 100 years of scientific progress. Special route markers guided visitors to the fair along the main thoroughfares leading to Chicago. Among the 14 marked routes were U.S. Route 12, the marine route; U.S. Route 20, the automotive route; and Route 66, the agricultural route. Visitors driving from downstate Illinois and the southwest would likely follow Route 66 and the agricultural route markers, featuring a farmer and plow, northeast through the Corn Belt.

Those with a knowledge of history might have understood that as they traveled the agricultural route, they were following the trail blazed by pioneering farmers nearly a century before. In New York, the 1825 opening of the Erie Canal created a navigable waterway between New York City and Lake Michigan. Thus from its incorporation as a town in 1833, Chicago was an emerging marketplace, poised to become a rival to St. Louis as the western gateway. According to Milo M. Quaife's book *Chicago's Highways Old and New*, along the corridor that would become Route 66, in seasons when the primitive path was passable, "a steady stream of wagons laden with the produce of the countryside" poured northeastward into Chicago. Wheat, corn, oats, and barley made their way to the docks along the Chicago River.

> In addition droves of cattle and hogs . . . wended their way by converging routes to their common doom in the slaughter yards of the incipient metropolis. . . . Returning, the wagons conveyed such supplies of coffee, salt, and groceries, stoves, crockery, or other merchandise as might be needed to supply the farmer's household, or perchance to replenish the retail stock of the storekeeper of his home community.

When the Illinois state legislature created Cook County in 1831, its land mass included most of the current six-county Chicago metropolitan area. The county population was 1,310, not including Native Americans. Quaife's book states that, to allow free passage of citizens to the county seat in unincorporated Chicago from the communities of Walker's Grove, just south of modern Plainfield, and Hickory Creek, near present-day Joliet, the county board "made provision for marking out the first two county highways of Cook County. . . . One of these roads ran on the line of . . . Ogden Avenue to the house of Barney Lawton at Riverside, and from thence to the house of James Walker, on the DuPage River, and so on to the west line of the County." Thus the corridor that would become Route 66 was an official county highway 95 years before the U.S. Highway system's creation. "Over this route, on January 1, 1834, was dispatched the first stagecoach which ever ran west out of Chicago. Its proprietor, Dr. John L. Temple, had secured the government contract for carrying the mail between Chicago and St. Louis."

Native Americans originally used this corridor because it was the shortest overland route between the navigable portions of the Chicago and Illinois Rivers. As early as 1673, French Canadian explorers Jacques Marquette and Louis Joliet had traveled by canoe up the local waterways to Lake Michigan. The difficulties of the journey through a slough known as Mud Lake led Joliet to write in his journal that the digging of a canal would create an unbroken waterway between the Illinois River and Lake Michigan. Wars, territorial disputes, and a lack of economic impetus kept the canal plans on the back burner until the completion of New York's Erie Canal changed the commercial landscape.

In 1848, the Illinois and Michigan Canal opened, giving Chicago a water route of commerce and transportation from Lake Michigan to the Illinois River at Ottawa. Especially in the winter months, when the canal closed to navigation, the Chicago-to-Walker's Grove county highway remained important for local transit, stagecoaches, and mail transportation. However, the *Chicago Tribune* stated that, "the road was regarded as having a grudge against every living thing—horse, ox, or man. Attempts to improve it by settling huge rocks for a foundation only served to draw new curses both on the road and on the citizens who tried to reform it." On the section from Ogden and Madison Streets in Chicago to Riverside, the Southwestern Plank Road Company received the franchise to build a single-track wooden roadbed. According to Quaife, "A four-horse vehicle paid 37½ cents toll for the privilege of traversing the ten mile highway; a single team paid 25 cents and a horse and rider half as much."

Chicago's first railroad—the Chicago and Galena Union—opened in 1848. The Chicago and Rock Island Railroad ran its first train from Chicago to Joliet in 1852, and by 1856, the Rock Island became the first railroad to bridge the Mississippi River. As the railway grew, it added the later Route 66 towns of Oklahoma City; Amarillo, Texas; and Tucumcari, New Mexico, to its litany of depots. In the years after the Civil War through the beginning of the 20th century, Chicago became the railroad capital of North America, and several other railways blazed an iron road through the Route 66 corridor. The Chicago and Alton Railroad connected through Joliet, Dwight, Bloomington, and Springfield to St. Louis. The Acheson, Topeka and Santa Fe Railroad stretched west from Chicago's Dearborn Station through Missouri, Kansas, and Colorado, then veered southward to connect Albuquerque with Flagstaff and Kingman, Arizona, and Needles, Barstow, San Bernardino, and Los Angeles, California.

The era of canals and rails saw the marginalization of road building. Farm-to-market roads in rural areas received cursory maintenance, enough to allow wagons to carry goods to the nearest canal port or rail depot. Urban thoroughfares ran the gamut from graded dirt, pine block, stone, or paving brick, depending upon the funds available to the community. Rail quickly became the preferred transportation mode for both local and long distance travel. The Chicago and Alton Railroad and Chicago, Burlington and Quincy Railroad provided commuter and interurban service along the Route 66 corridor in Illinois. In 1903, the Chicago, Rock Island and Pacific collaborated with the Southern Pacific on the *Golden State Limited* passenger service, which whisked travelers from Chicago to Los Angeles in 66 hours. Santa Fe's *Super Chief* and the *City of Los Angeles* trains operated by the Chicago and North Western and the Union Pacific

Railroads, also offered limited-stop service between the cities that would later be the terminal points of Route 66.

In addition to the passenger service offered by the long haul carriers, local street rail transit began in the Chicago area in 1859. Just after the 1871 Chicago fire, residents dislocated from the burned district flooded into the Route 66 corridor through the city's North Lawndale community and the near southwest suburbs of Cicero, Berwyn, Riverside, and Lyons. According to the *Chicago Tribune*, a horse-drawn streetcar line along Ogden Avenue started serving the new subdivisions prior to 1879; transit time from downtown to the west side was 41 minutes by one-horse power. Adams Street, which would become westbound Route 66 in 1953, was home to horsecars in 1885 and cable cars in 1893. The Adams Street and Ogden Avenue lines converted to electric trolley by 1906.

Street rail provided a convenient service at a nickel per trip for the working class; the merchant and upper class could afford to own a horse and carriage or to hire livery service as needed. Endeavors undertaken to reserve one urban thoroughfare for the exclusive use of light carriages bore fruit when Jackson Street was designated a Park Boulevard creating a grand carriageway between the lakefront Lake Park (later Grant Park) and the west side Garfield Park. Boulevards were off-limits to commercial traffic, which meant no "teaming" of heavy cartage wagons and no franchises for street rail. Boulevards were often much wider than other city streets and were among the first thoroughfares to be paved with asphalt. Due to their smooth riding surfaces, the boulevards became the favored routes for the "wheelmen"—the bicycling enthusiasts of the late 1800s.

The paving project on Jackson Boulevard began in 1892 west of the Chicago River in the jurisdiction of the West Park Commission. The *Chicago Tribune* stated that, "the roadway, forty-four feet wide, smooth as a marble mantel in a parlor, is one of the best bits of asphaltum work in the world." In August 1897, the South Park Commission completed their section, east of the river to Michigan Boulevard. According to the *Chicago Tribune*, "hundreds of bicyclists and scores of carriages and mail wagons tried the new asphalt and found it was good. . . . [Those] who used the boulevard last night called down blessings on the heads of the . . . Park Commissioners for the easy road to the West Side."

At the beginning of the 20th century, as those affluent enough to own their own horse and carriage traded them in for early horseless carriages, boulevards, including Jackson, remained the preferred thoroughfares for the Sunday drive. In 1900, there were 600 registered automobiles in the entire state of Illinois. That number grew to over 6,000 by 1905 and to over 15,000 in 1908. That year, the assembly-line production of the Ford Model T made motor touring affordable to the working class. The motoring enthusiast venturing beyond the boulevards into the rural hinterland surrounding Chicago encountered roads neglected for over half a century.

Historically road and bridge construction in Illinois was the responsibility of local government entities: municipalities, townships, and counties. In 1917, S. E. Brady, the state's superintendent of highways, wrote,

It was not until about 1911 that the people of the State of Illinois began to realize the condition of our highways as compared to other states and the handicap under which we were working. . . . Illinois, standing first in agriculture, second in wealth and third in population, occupied twenty-third place among the states of the union in the matter of highways which were improved.

To pull Illinois out of the mud, the state government went into the road-building business.

In 1916, the Illinois General Assembly passed "An Act to Construct Hard-Surfaced Roads upon the Public Highways." The act called for $60 million in bonds for the construction of the pavements with automobile registration fees earmarked to repay the debt. The Illinois Division of Highways issued 46 separate bond issues, with each paying for construction on a specified route. State Bond Issue (SBI) Route 4 provided funds for paving the route from Chicago to East

St. Louis, via Berwyn, Riverside, Lyons, Joliet, Dwight, Pontiac, Bloomington, Lincoln, Elkhart, Williamsville, Springfield, Carlinville, Edwardsville, and Granite City. By December 1926, motorists traveling from Chicago to St. Louis could follow markers for SBI Route 4 all the way through Illinois. They would find hard-surfaced roads from Jackson and Michigan Boulevards in Chicago to the Mississippi River crossing on the McKinley bridge at Venice.

On January 15, 1927, the United States Bureau of Public Roads officially announced a uniform numbering system for federal interstate highways. According to the *Chicago Tribune*, the 80,000-mile system's objective was to reach all parts of the country with roads "upon which motorists may start with complete confidence of smooth travel," and "to eliminate existing confusion as to route designations, markings, and safety signs." U.S. highway shields marked state roads expected to carry the major part of interstate traffic. Route 66 had a total mileage of 2,448, running from Chicago via Joliet, passing through St. Louis, and ending in Los Angeles. By the summer of 1928, Route 66 signs were in place along Illinois SBI Route 4.

According to Bobby Troup's classic song, "(Get Your Kicks on) Route 66," which was recorded by Nat King Cole, the highway was "the best" when taking a "California trip." However my family's commutes between paternal and maternal homesteads and our summer vacations took us no further west on the mother road than that visit to the Gateway Arch in St. Louis. One could start driving anywhere upon its length and travel in either direction from any point. Access was not limited, nor was there any limitation to the depth of a Route 66 experience.

Route 66 could be a corridor of travel to a destination, or it could function as the destination itself. Those with the latter point of view understand that history is not contained within museums, books, or memorial plaques. Our common history is everywhere, and clues to its meaning exist in every object in our built and natural environments. *Route 66 in Chicago* will take a closer look at the built environment along the highway's corridor in the metropolitan area. It will show how the structures along the road help symbolize and interpret the shared history of the city and the highway. The Route 66 journey begins in Chicago for reasons historic and contemporary, and commercial and utilitarian. It is time to get our kicks on Chicago's Route 66.

One

BEGINNING THE JOURNEY

From the beginning, the business of Chicago has been transportation. In 1829, the state legislature created the Illinois and Michigan Canal Commission to dig a waterway connecting the Chicago River with the Mississippi River by way of the Des Plaines and Illinois Rivers, and to lay out towns, sell lots, and apply the proceeds to the construction of the canal. The canal commissioners employed James Thompson, a civil engineer, to lay out the original town of Chicago. Incorporation as a town came in 1833 and as a city in 1837. Within 30 years, the city grew from a population of 100 to nearly 300,000 as Chicago took advantage of its water and railways to become the world's fastest growing commercial and manufacturing center.

Left behind in the rush to growth were amenities for the city's residents. In 1869, Chicago's lack of green space led the state legislature to create three park commissions that were charged with creating public parks in and around the city. Independent from municipal government, the commissions had, according to the *Chicago Tribune*, "the power to sue and be sued . . . and enjoy all powers necessary to govern, manage, and direct all parks, boulevards, and ways . . . to levy special assessments on all property deemed by them benefited . . . to select and take possession of, and acquire by condemnation, contract and donation, title, in trust for the public, to all land necessary" for parks and connecting boulevards.

The South Park Commission had charge of Michigan Boulevard from Twenty-second Street north to Lake Park along the downtown shoreline. By 1897, the South and West Park Commissions had made Jackson Street a boulevard, thus connecting Lake Park with the west side's Garfield Park. As motorists ventured onto the city's thoroughfares with their horseless carriages, they found the smooth asphalt of the park boulevards made for the most pleasant drives. Michigan and Jackson Boulevards were downtown Chicago's only streets devoid of streetcar tracks. Although the coming onslaught of automobiles would soon flood all streets in Chicago's grid, the intersection of the boulevards became this city of transportation's "route center"—the place where journeys began.

A word on nomenclature: thoroughfares under park jurisdiction are "boulevards" when connecting parks and "drives" within a park's boundaries. Thus Ogden Boulevard runs from Roosevelt Road southwest to Douglas Park, and Ogden Drive cuts diagonally through the park itself.

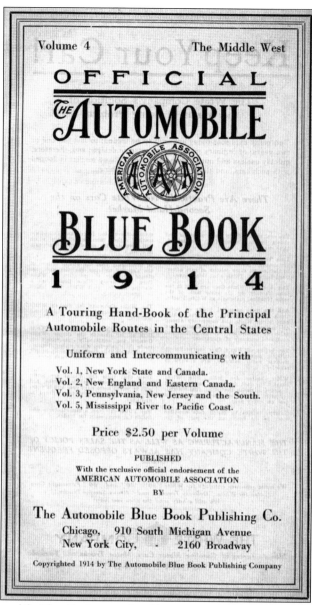

Volume 4 — The Middle West

OFFICIAL

THE AUTOMOBILE

BLUE BOOK

1 9 1 4

A Touring Hand-Book of the Principal
Automobile Routes in the Central States

Uniform and Intercommunicating with

Vol. 1, New York State and Canada.
Vol. 2, New England and Eastern Canada.
Vol. 3, Pennsylvania, New Jersey and the South.
Vol. 5, Mississippi River to Pacific Coast.

Price $2.50 per Volume

PUBLISHED
With the exclusive official endorsement of the
AMERICAN AUTOMOBILE ASSOCIATION
BY

The Automobile Blue Book Publishing Co.

Chicago, 910 South Michigan Avenue
New York City, - 2160 Broadway

Copyrighted 1914 by The Automobile Blue Book Publishing Company

The *Official Automobile Blue Book* started publication in 1901, giving motorists in the early automobile age a handbook of the principal automobile routes in the United States and Canada. In the years before named automobile trails or numbered highways, the book was indispensable for inter-city travel. Twenty miles from Chicago on the route to Bloomington, the directions in the 1914 volume state, "Diagonal 4-corners, sign on far right; bear right with heavy poles on fine stone, going straight ahead thru all crossroads, running onto rough gravel." Within Chicago, all book routes began at the "route center." "All routes starting from Chicago are begun at the intersection of Jackson and Michigan Boulevards, for this is not only the central point north and south, but Jackson Boulevard . . . is the only street offering a suitable exit east and west through the city, therefore practically all travel in any direction must use either Jackson or Michigan Boulevard. In addition to this, it is within two blocks of the heart of the city . . . and within easy reach of all the principal downtown hotels."

CHICAGO'S WATER FRONT.

This view shows Chicago's downtown waterfront, looking west between 1904 and 1910. The tallest building in the center of the view is the Railway Exchange Building and on the left is the Stratford Hotel. Jackson Boulevard runs west between the Stratford Hotel and the Railway Exchange Building, and Michigan Boulevard parallels the lakeshore in front of both buildings. The plume of smoke to the right of the Railway Exchange Building emanates from a locomotive of the Illinois Central Railroad, whose tracks were located at the water's edge. Between the tracks and Michigan Boulevard, Grant Park (known as Lake Park until 1901), a narrow strip of green, stretched 10 blocks south (left) from Jackson Boulevard to Twelfth Street. Travelers taking Jackson Boulevard west from Michigan Boulevard encountered Garfield Park, four miles distant and directly on Jackson Boulevard, or they could travel two miles and then veer left onto Ogden Avenue for a visit to Douglas Park. From 1910 through 1933, Chicago's skyline and lakefront saw dramatic changes, but Michigan and Jackson Boulevards remained the preferred automobile routes in the downtown area for through traffic.

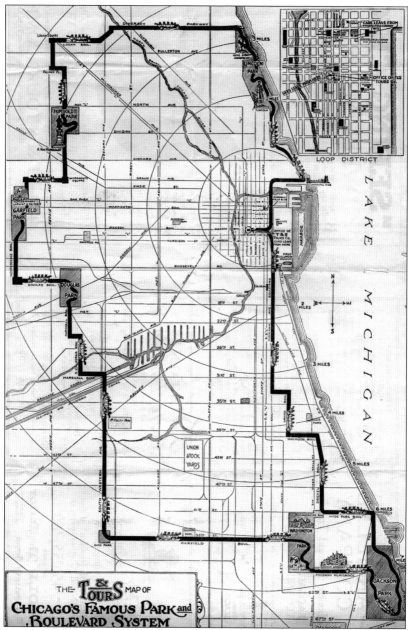

The *Official Automobile Blue Book* of 1918 states, "No automobile tourist should leave the city without making at least a partial circuit of the boulevard system, which is so arranged that many round trips can be taken, varying in length from 15 to 60 miles, taking in most of the parks of which the city is so justly proud. A trip of this character is almost a necessity to give the stranger an idea not only of the enormous area of the city, but to properly realize the great work that has been accomplished to change what was originally a swamp into one of the most attractive cities in the U.S." This 1920 map is from a Chicago tour company that offered a "De Luxe Tour of the Park and Boulevard System" along the outer circle of boulevards. Garfield Park is at the far left of the map above center, and Douglas Park is below and slightly to the right of Garfield Park. Grant Park is at the far right of the map above center.

Douglas Park, Refectory and Boat House, Chicago.
One of the West Side Parks; Area 182 Acres.

These two postcards show structures in Douglas Park visible from Ogden Drive (Route 66 through Chicago's West Side). After its creation in 1869, park improvements in the 19th century developed slowly and included a 26-acre lagoon and boathouse (above). The park fell into severe neglect and disrepair by 1905, when a $2 million West Park restoration and improvement program began. Landscape architect Jens Jenson built the prairie-style Lily Pond and Pavilion (right) at the southeast corner of Ogden and Sacramento Drives. A fieldhouse replaced the boathouse in 1928; the pavilion remains intact after a 2001 restoration.

291.   LILY POND AND PAVILION, DOUGLAS PARK, CHICAGO.

50291

OGDEN BOULEVARD, CHICAGO

One of the many pretty boulevards on the west side of the city.

These postcard views show Chicago's west side boulevards in the eventual Route 66 corridor, both from about 1907. Ogden Boulevard (above) ran southwest towards Douglas Park. Grass parkways separated a center driveway for through two-way traffic and streetcars from one-way side drives. When the West Park Commission assumed control of Ogden Boulevard in the 1890s, existing streetcar lines, originally franchised along the thoroughfare in the 1870s, continued to operate. Ashland Boulevard (below) is seen looking north from Jackson Boulevard. The Near West Side was home to a large upper-middle-class community in the 1870s–1900s. Local residents included Mary Todd Lincoln and famed private detective William A. Pinkerton. In 1893, a disgruntled citizen murdered Chicago mayor Carter Harrison in the mayor's home on Ashland Boulevard south of Jackson Boulevard. During the Route 66 era, Ashland Boulevard became a commercial and retail thoroughfare.

ASHLAND BOULEVARD, CHICAGO

Looking north from Jackson Boulevard, west side. One of Chicago's most beautiful residence streets.

The 1872 hotel at the southwest corner of Jackson and Michigan Boulevards was designed by architect William W. Boyington and started life as the Gardner House. According to Rand McNally's 1893 *Bird's-Eye Views and Guide to Chicago*, the hotel "was always noticeable for the varying bright colors with which its walls were covered." The Gardner House, a showplace of the Chicago lakefront, featured a courtyard filled with flowers and a facade with Second Empire design elements. In 1880, new owners renamed it the Leland Hotel. The *Chicago Tribune* stated that "many prominent men frequented it and it was known widely for its excellent cuisine and service." One guest of the hotel was John L. Sullivan, heavyweight boxing champion from 1882–1892. In 1902, it changed hands again, becoming the Stratford Hotel. These postcard views show the Stratford's exterior and interior about 1907.

LOBBY
STRATFORD HOTEL
CHICAGO

The Stratford Hotel (right) helped establish the Jackson Boulevard corridor as a thoroughfare with ample amenities for visitors to Chicago. By the 1890s, Jackson Boulevard and its adjacent streets were home to a dozen hotels, including the Richelieu Hotel (left of the Stratford Hotel), built on Michigan Boulevard in 1885. After 1909, larger and more modern hotels began to compete with the Richelieu and Stratford Hotels. Cognizant of the changing hotel business, the owners of the Stratford Hotel made bold plans in 1914 to build a new 260-foot-tall showplace. The new hotel would retain some Second Empire features, including a mansard roof. However, an ordinance restricted building height to 200 feet, and the city council denied the developers' request for a variance. The old Stratford Hotel remained until finally closing in 1922. A 1918 adaptive reuse project renovated the Richelieu Hotel for office and retail use; it remains standing with a much-altered facade. As seen in this photograph taken between 1912 and 1918, motorcars could park in the center of wider thoroughfares such as Michigan Boulevard in the early motor age.

RAILWAY EXCHANGE BUILDING, CHICAGO

No. 177. V. O. Hammon Pub. Co., Chicago

The 1904 Railway Exchange Building stands at the northwest corner of Jackson and Michigan Boulevards. The Wellington Hotel is visible to the left in this postcard view from between 1907 and 1915. The Railway Exchange Building housed the main offices of many Chicago-based railroad companies, including the Chicago and Alton and the Acheson, Topeka and Santa Fe. At 17 stories, it was one of the tallest buildings along Michigan Boulevard at the beginning of the 20th century and, according to the *Chicago Tribune*, railway companies moved into it "in the fond belief that they would escape much of the noise and grime of downtown Chicago." After relocating to the Railway Exchange, railroad moguls were in the ironic position of complaining about the clatter and smoke emanating from the lakefront tracks of the Illinois Central Railroad. Their complaints joined the chorus of other lakefront office workers and landowners, who called for the Illinois Central to lower their tracks below grade and electrify the line in the downtown area. The Illinois Central finally succumbed to the public outcry and completed the changes in 1926.

BROOKINS IN HIS AEROPLANE OVER ART INSTITUTE AND GRANT PARK, CHICAGO.

These postcards show two aerial views of Michigan Boulevard looking north. The postcard on the left shows the biplane of Walter Brookins flying over Grant Park. Jackson Boulevard extends west (left) near the horizontal centerline of the image. On September 27 and 28, 1910, Brookins made four short flights over Chicago, taking off and landing in Grant Park. On September 29, Brookins flew from Chicago to Springfield, winning a $10,000 prize for the longest one-day flight at that time. Tailing along in a special Illinois Central train was Wilbur Wright of the Wright Brothers, the builders of Brookins's airplane. The 188-mile trip took 7 hours and 10 minutes with two stops. In the c. 1921 postcard below, the Illinois Central lakefront tracks on the right are shown below grade, and some of the improvements to Grant Park are evident.

252. MICHIGAN BOULEVARD, LOOKING NORTH, SEEN FROM AEROPLANE, CHICAGO. THE DRAKE.

THE BLACKSTONE.

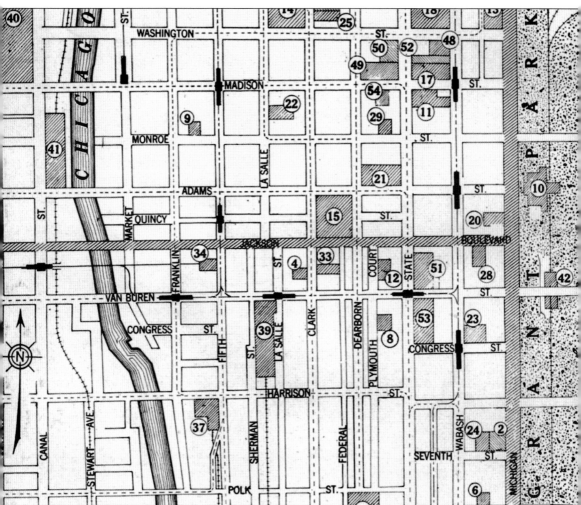

This map from the 1918 *Official Automobile Blue Book* shows Jackson Boulevard running horizontally in the middle of the image, and Michigan Boulevard running vertically on the right, just west of Grant Park. Number 42 on the map is the Van Buren Street Station of the Illinois Central Railroad; from here, one sees that the park now stretches east of the Illinois Central tracks on new landfill. Dotted lines in the middle of city thoroughfares other than Jackson and Michigan Boulevards indicate the routes of streetcar lines in the downtown district. Jackson Boulevard became an important thoroughfare for travelers because it was near most of the important rail depots, including Union Station (41), Aurora and Elgin (34), Grand Central (37), and LaSalle Street Station (39). Nightlife for visitors and residents was available at nearby theaters, including the Auditorium (23), the Illinois (28), and the Princess (33). In 1918, Jackson Boulevard was home to the Stratford, Grand Pacific, Great Northern, Atlantic, and Grace Hotels. All the hotels offered fine dining, and other eateries along the street included Bennert's, Pixley and Ehlers, Thompson's, and Raklios Restaurants.

These two postcards show early traffic control equipment at the "route center" intersection of Jackson and Michigan Boulevards. The top postcard is from about 1916; the bottom is from about 1922. According to an August 29, 1920, article in the *Chicago Tribune*, a traffic check conducted by B. F. Goodrich Company statisticians found 36,665 automobiles passing through the intersection in a 12-hour period. "The recorders, who are conducting similar checks in other cities, state the intersection of these two thoroughfares will come close to landing the title of 'America's most intensely traveled corner.'" It was "a greater number of cars than those registered in any one of the following entire states during 1919: Arizona, Delaware, New Hampshire, New Mexico, Nevada, Utah, Vermont, Wyoming." The company's workers noted motor vehicles with license plates from "practically every state in the union" passing through the intersection.

MICHIGAN BOULEVARD, SHOWING TRAFFIC TOWER, CHICAGO   113

The Stratford Hotel succumbed to the wrecking ball in 1922, eight years after the owner's plans to build a new 260-foot structure failed to get approval. Ironically the building that replaced the Stratford Hotel in 1924 was 32 stories and 475 feet in height. A 1923 zoning change allowed buildings taller than 200 feet if the upper floors were set back to help sunlight reach the adjoining streets. The new building at the southwest corner of Michigan and Jackson Boulevards, one of the first to take advantage of the new ordinance, was the Midwest headquarters of S. W. Straus and Company. An investment-banking firm whose motto was "42 Years without Loss to Any Investor," Straus and Company was renowned for selling secure first mortgage bonds that financed the construction of hundreds of buildings, including the Ambassador Hotel chain. A pyramid roof, symbolizing longevity, topped the building's nine-story tower. At the apex, a glass beehive housed a directional beacon. The beehive stood for industry and thrift, and the beacon symbolized the global reach of the Straus firm.

These two photographs, showing the view from atop the Straus Building looking north along Michigan Boulevard, highlight changes to the Chicago skyline that occurred in the last half of the 1920s. Both images show the Peoples Gas Building in the near foreground. Further north on the west side of Michigan Boulevard in the 1926 photograph at left are the Montgomery Ward and Wrigley Buildings. The tallest skyscrapers on the horizon are the 1926 Jeweler's Building (left) and the 1925 Tribune Tower (right). Dominating the skyline in the photograph below, taken from the same vantage point at least three years later, are the 1927 Pittsfield Building (38 stories, 557 feet tall) on the left, and the 1929 Willoughby Tower (36 stories, 448 feet tall) on the right. The slender 1928 Mather Tower is in the center background, left of the Willoughby.

Continental Companies Building
Michigan Ave., at
Jackson Blvd.,
Chicago

Prior to 1924, S. W. Straus and Company offered only high-quality first-mortgage bonds and other issues of similar safety. During the 1920s building boom, they began financing the construction of skyscrapers with junior liens secured only by the character and earnings power of the borrower. If a building they financed fell through, Straus simply sold more bonds, and then paid the interest and principal of the previous investors from the sales to newcomers. Salespersons for the company sold these bonds without disclosing that they were not the safe first-mortgage bonds for which the company was famous. Unfortunately the virtual shutdown of the building and construction industry during the Great Depression gave the pyramid roof on the Chicago Straus Building a completely new meaning: Pyramid Scheme. Lawsuits and receivership spelled the end of S. W. Straus and Company. The rooftop symbols of longevity, industry, thrift, and global reach would prove to be more fitting for Route 66 than for Straus. This 1944 postcard shows that the building at Jackson and Michigan Boulevards had become home to the Continental Insurance Companies, later known as CNA.

Starting in 1916, Chicago created new parkland east of the Illinois Central tracks with clay and dirt excavated from construction sites and underground tunneling projects. In 1926, the Illinois Central Railroad completed their project to lower their tracks below grade and operate all moving stock via electric power instead of steam locomotive. The expanded Grant Park became Chicago's lakefront emerald jewel. The road in this aerial view running diagonally through Grant Park, from the Continental Insurance (formerly Straus) and Railway Exchange Buildings (above center, left) to the lower right corner, is Jackson Drive. Finished in 1933, this eastward extension of Jackson Boulevard ran four-tenths of a mile from Michigan Boulevard and connected to the new Outer Drive, out of view to the right. Completion of the Outer Drive in 1937 allowed the Illinois Division of Highways to reroute U.S. Route 41 off congested Michigan Boulevard. The terminus of U.S. Routes 66 and 34 (which also utilized Jackson through downtown Chicago) moved in 1937 as well in order to maintain a connection with Route 41.

This 1941 photograph shows the view looking west down Jackson Drive from the Outer Drive. The westbound starting point and eastbound terminus of U.S. Routes 66 and 34 moved to this intersection in 1937, when the opening of the Outer Drive bridge over the Chicago River completed the city's lakefront thoroughfare. In the center background, the silhouettes of the Continental Insurance and Railway Exchange Buildings mark the original 1926–1936 starting point of Route 66. John Vachon, a photographer employed by the Federal Office of War Information, took this photograph as part of a project documenting Americans at work and play on the home front and their mobilization efforts for World War II. The Outer Drive from downtown to Chicago's south side carried various names during its piecemeal construction, including East Drive, Field Drive, and Leif Eriksen Drive. The north side Lincoln Park Commission called their portion of the lakefront thoroughfare Lake Shore Drive, and in 1946 that name became the official moniker for the entire drive. (Courtesy Library of Congress, Prints and Photographs Division.)

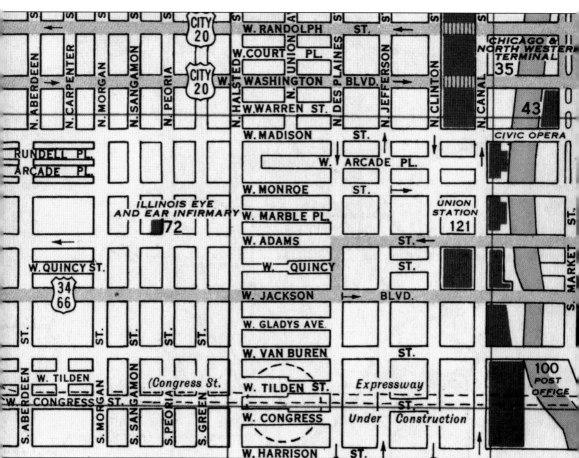

Financial difficulties of Chicago's separate park commissions during the Great Depression led to consolidation into a single entity called the Chicago Park District, which retained jurisdiction of the park boulevards. In 1951, to ease downtown traffic flow, streets under Chicago municipal control parallel to Jackson Boulevard became one-way thoroughfares. Randolph, Madison, and Adams Street handled westbound traffic, while Monroe and Washington became eastbound only. In January 1953, the park district made Jackson Boulevard one way eastbound from

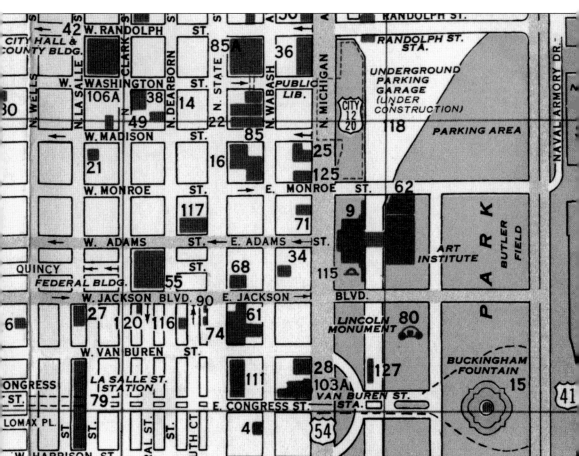

Desplaines Street to Michigan Boulevard. Jackson Drive east of Michigan Boulevard remained a two-way thoroughfare. This Conoco Oil map, made by H. M. Gousha Company, shows how the change affected U.S. Routes 66 and 34. Westbound traffic traveled west on Jackson Boulevard from Lake Shore Drive to Michigan Boulevard, north on Michigan Boulevard to Adams Street, west on Adams Street to Desplaines Street, then south on Desplaines Street to rejoin Jackson Boulevard and continue west.

This July 1940 photograph shows the view north on Michigan Boulevard from Jackson Boulevard. This is where westbound Route 66 traffic would turn north due to the January 1953 routing changes. City and park district officials considered the one-way designations successful in smoothing downtown traffic flow, so the program expanded in October 1953. One way eastbound Jackson started three miles further west near Garfield Park at Campbell Avenue, so the section of the boulevard utilized by U.S. Routes 66 and 34 was entirely one way from Ogden Avenue to Michigan Boulevard. Consequently westbound traffic for the highways remained on Adams Street from Michigan Boulevard all the way to Ogden Avenue as well. Ogden continued to handle two-way traffic for both highways in Chicago's Near West Side and North Lawndale communities as well as in Cicero and Berwyn. No other routing changes occurred on Route 66 in Chicago during the rest of its official life as a commissioned highway. (Photograph by John Vachon, courtesy Library of Congress, Prints and Photographs Division.)

With the 1953 rerouting of westbound Route 66, the Art Institute of Chicago (above, in a 1917 postcard view) became part of the highway's corridor. This 1893 building was one of the first improvements in the area west of Michigan Boulevard that would become Grant Park in 1901. Although built to be the permanent home to the institute, the building's first use was for meetings and displays for the Columbian Exposition, Chicago's 1893 worlds fair. The postcard at right shows the 1911 Peoples Gas Light and Coke Company building, located at the northwest corner of Adams Street and Michigan Boulevard as seen from Grant Park south of the Art Institute of Chicago. D. H. Burnham and Company, the same architectural firm responsible for the Railway Exchange Building at Jackson and Michigan Boulevards, designed this structure to house the main offices of the local natural gas utility company.

232. PEOPLES GAS LIGHT AND COKE CO·S. BUILDING AND

GREAT LAKES FOUNTAIN AT ART INSTITUTE, CHICAGO.

Pulman Bldg., Chicago, Ill.

The 1883 building in this postcard view, designed by architect Solon S. Beman, stood at the southwest corner of Adams Street and Michigan Boulevard until 1956. The building housed the downtown offices of the Pullman Palace Car Company, manufacturers of railroad sleeping cars. Beman also designed Pullman's factory and company town south of Chicago (annexed into the city in 1889). Unusual for tall downtown buildings of the late 19th century, the Pullman building included residential apartments as well as office and retail space. Broadway showman Flo Ziegfeld resided here whenever theater business brought him to Chicago. Route 66 travelers heading west down Adams Street past the Pullman building from 1953 to 1956 in their motorcars likely took little note that they were passing the company that built the sleeping cars in which their fathers and grandmothers had traveled. As a sign of the changing eras, the Pullman building's demolition in 1956 made way for the headquarters of the Borg-Warner Corporation, one of the nation's largest automotive parts manufacturers. Yet no matter the method of transport, the journeys began from Chicago's route center.

Two

CREATING
THE CORRIDOR

The French visitors started out from the shore of Lake Michigan, bound on an American adventure with the goal of reaching the Pacific Ocean. Over the years since the highway's creation, many visitors from distant lands have come to partake in this journey from lake to sea via Route 66. They encounter the mighty Mississippi River, and they meet Native Americans who keep the centuries-old traditions of their ancestors alive. Some travel the entire distance of over 2,000 miles; others never reach the Pacific Ocean yet find fulfillment in the journey nonetheless.

Although they shared the goal of reaching the Pacific Ocean, this particular group of Frenchmen differed from other travelers in several ways. Instead of heading west in automobiles or on motorcycles on a ribbon of asphalt and concrete, these travelers made their way by boat and on foot. They had no maps and no knowledge of what might lie ahead of them. Two men, named Jacques Marquette and Louis Joliet, led them; the year was 1673.

Their trip via Green Bay, the Fox River, and an overland portage to the Wisconsin River got them to the Mississippi River and southward to the Arkansas River. Realizing they were approaching lands claimed by Spain, with who France was at war, they decided to return home; although they were far from their goal of reaching the Pacific Ocean, they noted that the Arkansas or Missouri Rivers might prove to be the sought-for water link to the western ocean.

On the return trip to Canada, the voyageurs' native guide suggested a shorter route. They traveled north on the Mississippi River, then followed the Illinois and Des Plaines Rivers. Between the Des Plaines and Chicago Rivers, a low ridge divided the watershed of the Mississippi River system from the Great Lakes system. They traversed a slough across the ridge; and from the Chicago River, the explorers paddled back to Lake Michigan and on to Canada. They reported on their explorations and wrote about their journey. In so doing, they germinated the concept of a transportation corridor connecting Chicago to the Mississippi River and the West.

The passage where pioneers traveled from the Des Plaines to the Chicago River became known as the Chicago Portage. The statue shown above, erected in 1989, commemorates the portage site with a depiction of Jacques Marquette and Louis Joliet's 1673 voyage. The map below shows the route from the Des Plaines River to Lake Michigan. Canoes of 12-inch draft or less could usually navigate the passage 45 days out of the year. In dry weather, Mud Lake was a quagmire. According to Milo M. Quaife's book *Chicago's Highways Old and New*, early Chicago settler Gurdon Hubbard wrote, "This lake was . . . but a scum of liquid mud, a foot or more deep, over which our boats were slid, not floated over, men wading each side . . . often sinking deep in this filthy mire, filled with bloodsuckers. . . . Three days were consumed in passing through this sinkhole of . . . two miles in length."

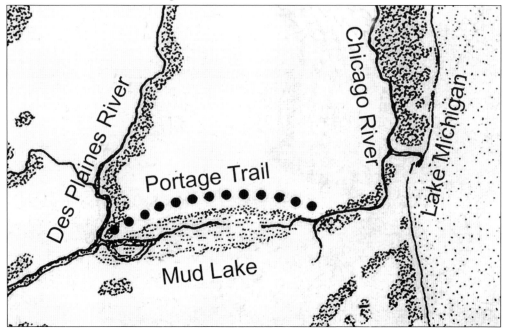

These photographs show close-ups of Louis Joliet (above) and Jacques Marquette (below) from the iron sculpture that stands at the Chicago Portage National Historic Site on Harlem Avenue south of Forty-seventh Street. The explorers were the first non-natives to write about their travel across the portage, although there is evidence that French Canadian fur traders may have known of the passage prior to 1673. According to Quaife, in his journal "Louis Joliet suggested the digging of a canal through Mud Lake would create an unbroken waterway between the Illinois River and Lake Michigan." However Joliet's visit in the wet season gave a false sense of the navigability of the upper Des Plaines River. A 1721 account by a French missionary indicated that he saw a bison fording the river at a spot so shallow "that the water barely reached its knees."

1409   *Marquette Building, Chicago, Ill.*

This postcard shows the 1895 Marquette Building, located in Chicago at the northwest corner of Adams and Dearborn Streets. The architects were Holabird and Roche, who incorporated themes into the entryway and lobby celebrating the importance of Jacques Marquette in the history and growth of the Chicago region. In the *AIA Guide to Chicago*, Timothy Wittman wrote, "Owen F. Aldis, a real estate developer, amateur historian, and one of the building's original owners, had translated Marquette's journal in 1891, providing the inspiration for the structure's name and decorative program." The two-story lobby features carved marble and mosaics showing scenes from Marquette's adventures, designed by J. A. Holzer and executed by the Tiffany Glass and Decorating Company. The building became part of the Route 66 corridor in 1953, when Adams Street first handled westbound highway traffic. The Marquette Building's current owners meticulously restored the external facade, and they welcome visitors wishing to admire the lobby's ornamentation. Placed on the National Register of Historic Places in 1973, the Marquette Building was named a Chicago landmark in 1975. It once housed offices of over 30 railroad companies.

"TO FOLLOW THOSE WATERS * * * WHICH WILL HENCEFORTH LEAD VS INTO STRANGE LANDS"

The top photograph shows one of the bas-relief panels located above the entry doors of the Marquette Building. Herman A. MacNeil sculpted the panels, and the plaques beneath them have quotes from Marquette's travel journal. MacNeil's work is also evident on the entryway's revolving doors, which feature tomahawks and panther heads. The sculpture of Marquette (right) is one of a dozen bronze busts above the elevator doors in the building's lobby. Other subjects depicted include Louis Joliet, Native Americans, and indigenous animals that the explorers encountered during their journey. Edward Kemys was the artist; he was a self-taught sculptor that specialized in Native American and animal subjects. His most famous work includes the lion statues located in front of the Art Institute of Chicago.

MARQUETTE

Several overland Native American trails converged near the Chicago Portage, since in dry weather the shallow Des Plaines River in this vicinity made for easy fording. Brothers Bernardus and David Laughton built their trading post in 1828 near the ford that bears their name. The above stone marks the location of the Laughton Trading House. The Cook County Forest Preserve map below shows U.S. Routes 66 and 34 (which was the 1926–1928 alignment of Route 66). Both of these highways follow the general corridor of Native American trails, which were the most direct overland paths between Lake Michigan and the deeper waters of the lower Illinois River at Ottawa and LaSalle. The numbers on the map show the locations of Stoney Ford (3), Laughton's Ford and Trading Post (5 and 6), and the Chicago Portage National Historic Site (7).

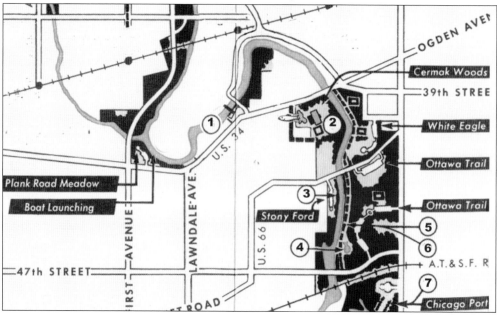

CHICAGO IN 1820.

The above postcard depicts Chicago in 1820. The north (right) and south (left) forks of the Chicago River flowed sluggishly and joined at the main branch, then meandered east toward Lake Michigan (foreground). Mud Lake and the Chicago Portage were located at the far end of the south fork. In the distance is the flat tall-grass prairie, which is interrupted only by small stands of trees on higher ground next to river bends. The small settlement near the river mouth on the south bank is the second Fort Dearborn, built in 1816. In the 1840s, after total expenditures nearing $250,000, improvement to the harbor of Chicago allowed lake vessels to moor at docks along the riverbanks. The photograph below shows the Illinois and Michigan Canal in Lockport. The canal created a water transport link between Chicago and the Mississippi River.

The view at left shows the Illinois and Michigan Canal's lock No. 1, located south of Lockport. Wooden gates at the ends of the lock channels controlled water levels in each of the canal's 16 locks. Barges traveled from Bridgeport in Chicago to LaSalle and Peru in 20–25 hours. Passenger packet boats brought thousands of travelers through the canal until the Chicago, Rock Island and Pacific Railroad completed their tracks from Chicago to Peru in 1853. The canal continued operation into the railroad era for shipment of lumber, coal, stone, and grain. Mules that followed a towpath along the edge of the canal towed the barges. The photograph below marks the location of the towpath in Summit. Later an early alignment of Illinois SBI Route 4 crossed the towpath at this same location.

This 1938 aerial view shows the street grid of the village of Lyons in the upper left quarter of the image, and the village of Summit in the lower right corner. The Des Plaines River snakes around Lyons, starting on the top left and flowing northeast, then meandering south, then southwest just below the centerline of the image. To the right of the Des Plaines River near the center of this view, Mud Lake was woodland by 1938. Flowing from the bottom center northeast, the widest waterway in the image is the Illinois Sanitary and Ship Canal, a deeper and wider passage completed in 1900. The ship canal changed the region's natural topography and lowered the water table. Mud Lake dried up; the reclaimed land became forest preserve on the east bank of the Des Plaines River and the village of Stickney east of Harlem Avenue (the north–south road near the right edge of the image.) The Illinois and Michigan Canal is a thin line parallel and below the ship canal. The two diagonal roads near the top were both Route 66 during the highway's existence.

After the completion of the Illinois Sanitary and Ship Canal, the Illinois and Michigan Canal fell into disuse. Additional land reclamation and flood control was the goal of another project that deepened the Des Plaines River and placed concrete levees along its course. The above photograph shows the embankments and the Hofmann Dam, just north of the original Route 66 alignment through Lyons. Where the Des Plaines River could once be easily forded, bridges were now required. The Ottawa, or Portage Trail, the main overland route used before canal building times, became the Southwestern Plank Road in 1848, and it was renamed Ogden Avenue in 1872. Route 66 first crossed the Des Plaines River in 1926–1928 on a two-lane bridge built in 1911. The photograph below shows a four-lane Ogden Avenue bridge, built in 1938.

During the 1925 construction season, the Illinois Division of Highways built the bridge in the above photograph as a new alignment of Joliet Road over the Des Plaines River for SBI Route 4, and soon Route 66. It was standard practice at the time to build a bridge one season before completing the connecting roadbed and approaches. However the 1926 construction season was marked with political squabbling between the state, which intended to build all highways leading to Chicago as two-lane thoroughfares, and Cook County, which was insisting on four-lane roads due to the higher traffic demands of the metropolitan area. The bridge remained an orphan in the woods until completion of the new four-lane pavement between August and December 1928. The photograph below shows the current Joliet Road bridge over the Des Plaines River as seen from Stoney Ford in the Cook County Forest Preserve.

The early commercial success of Chicago depended upon the navigability of the Chicago River, which ran through the heart of the city and separated the business district from the north and west sides. River crossings by foot, horse, or rail were nonstop, as was the river traffic. Bridges had to accommodate the frequent passage of masted ships. These photographs show the 1888 Jackson Boulevard bridge (above) and the 1889 Adams Street bridge (left). Both were steam-driven swing bridges, which would pivot 90 degrees to allow ships to pass. The *Chicago Tribune* called the Jackson Boulevard bridge "the show structure of Chicago . . . [with] two roadways, each twenty-one feet wide, and two six-foot wide sidewalks." A weakness of the swing bridge design was the need for a pier for the central pivot, which narrowed the navigation channel.

The Jack Knife bridge (above) was located south of the Jackson Boulevard bridge; it was one of the first bascule bridges in downtown Chicago. The Jack Knife bridge carried trains for the Metropolitan West Side Elevated Railroad. The postcard below shows the Jackson Boulevard Strauss trunnion bascule bridge, which replaced the Jackson Boulevard swing bridge in 1916. A trunnion is a shaft, or pivot-point, and bascule is the French word for seesaw. A counterweight located below deck level on the riverbank balances the weight of each leaf of the bridge. A complex of gears and electric motors, operated by a bridge tender, pivots the counterweight downward and the bridge leaf upward and away from the center of the river. Joseph Strauss, who later was the chief engineer for the construction of the Golden Gate Bridge, patented this design.

The image above is from *American Review of Reviews* of March 1918. The accompanying article states, "Chicago . . . has been . . . the greatest inland water transportation center in the world." In the late 19th century, the harbor at Chicago handled more ships than "New York, San Francisco, Philadelphia, Baltimore, Charleston, and Mobile combined," despite being closed to navigation in the winter months. The postcard below shows the steamboat *Roosevelt* passing through the State Street bridge around 1914. Passenger ships providing service from Chicago to points in Wisconsin and Michigan along the Lake Michigan shoreline continued to operate long after the transfer of most cargo traffic to Calumet Harbor in 1906. In the 1930s, the completion of the Illinois Waterway created a modern water link between the Illinois and Calumet Rivers via a widened and deepened Des Plaines River channel.

The above image is from a stereo view slide from about 1926 or 1927, looking south along the Chicago River. A gravel barge passes the site where the new Adams Street bascule bridge is under construction. Then-new Union Station is in the background. The 1940s aerial view below looks north along the same section of the river. Union Station is on the left, and shown top to bottom are the Adams Street, Jackson Boulevard, and Jack Knife bridges. The Jackson Boulevard bascule bridge is one of the oldest spans still in use on Route 66. The Adams Street and Jackson Boulevard bridges in Chicago and the Ruby Street bridge in Joliet are the only movable span bridges on the entire length of Route 66. Demolition of the Jack Knife bridge occurred when the rapid transit rail line it served moved to a new subway in the 1950s.

More tour boats and pleasure craft than cargo barges now use the Chicago River. During the April 15–November 15 boating season, over 50,000 ships still use the river, requiring 30,000 bridge openings each year. The city requested and received restrictions from the federal government, so now the bridges will only open during nonpeak traffic hours, and only with 12–48 hours advance request. The photograph above shows a flotilla of sailboats traveling from winter dry docks to their lakefront moorings. The aerial view below shows Route 66 running east towards its beginning point at Lake Shore Drive. Beyond the lakefront, pleasure craft can be seen at their summer moorings in Monroe Harbor. Monroe Harbor can accommodate approximately 1,000 boats and is one of nine harbors along Chicago's lakefront. (Above, courtesy of Carl Johnson.)

Structures with a water theme are scattered along Chicago's Route 66 corridor. The 1913 Spirit of the Great Lakes Fountain (above) is located next to the Art Institute of Chicago at the northeast corner of Jackson and Michigan Boulevards. Sculpted by Lorado Taft, the fountain's five female figures represent the Great Lakes. Water flows from shells held by the figures in the same way that it passes through the lakes: Lake Superior at the top and Lake Michigan on the side empty their water into the basin held by Lake Huron, who sends the stream on to Lakes Erie and Ontario. The postcard below shows boaters on holiday in Douglas Park around 1915. The lagoon served aesthetic and recreational purposes but was also functional; it helped drain the rest of the parkland, which had been a swampy prairie.

Buckingham Fountain is located between Lake Shore and Columbus Drives, which was at the starting point of Route 66 from 1937 to 1977. The 1927 fountain is a metaphorical celebration of Lake Michigan. Four "sea horse" creatures surround a raised basin symbolizing the four states surrounding the lake. The central jet pulses periodically to a height of 135 feet, and lights bathe the fountain in changing colors at night. The 1952 postcard above used the fountain to promote Gray Line Tours, a company that continues to offer bus tours for visiting tourists. The 1964 postcard below shows the illuminated fountain at night with a backdrop of the Chicago skyline. From Lake Michigan through rivers, wetlands, portages, or canals, pioneering Americans forged a transportation corridor born of water. Industrial advancements would change the method of transport; but the corridor, once created, proved adaptable to the changes.

Three

EXPANDING
THE GATEWAY

In 1803, Pres. Thomas Jefferson purchased the Louisiana Territory from France, and he commissioned Lewis and Clark to chart the uncharted. Pioneers flooded west by many routes, but the most popular corridor in the first 25 years of the 19th century was a journey by boat along the Ohio River then upriver on the Mississippi River to St. Louis. The original gateway to the great American West, St. Louis was where travelers paused to gather provisions for the rest of their journey, and it was where dealers for eastern markets purchased goods produced in the west.

In 1825, the completion of the Erie Canal changed the commercial geography. Suddenly the economic juggernaut of New York City had access to an unbroken waterway from the Hudson River, the new canal, and the Great Lakes, to the frontier outpost known as Chicago. Almost immediately, some farmers in central Illinois and Indiana began bringing their goods north to Chicago instead of west to St. Louis. With the Illinois and Michigan Canal still 23 years away, the Chicago market was reached via the existing overland trails; the most heavily traveled was the Ottawa Trail, the eventual corridor of Route 66.

The completion of the Illinois and Michigan Canal converted more of St. Louis's northeastern hinterland into Chicago's tributary area. As Chicago-based railroads pushed west to the Mississippi River, towns along the upper river valley from Minneapolis to Quincy diverted their goods to the Windy City. The Chicago, Rock Island and Pacific; Chicago and North Western; Illinois Central; and Chicago, Burlington and Quincy Railroads all bridged the Mississippi River by 1868 and forged further west, positioning themselves for connection to the coming transcontinental railroad. Riverboat operators used their political influence to block attempts to build rail bridges near St. Louis, and they fought losing legal battles to stop the upriver crossings.

The 1874 Eads bridge finally gave St. Louis a rail link to the east. It was too little, too late. The city by the lake's superior connections to the Pacific Ocean and New York meant a transfer of title: Chicago was the new gateway to the great American West.

This map shows the main passenger railroad lines serving the Route 66 corridor. On the northernmost route, the Chicago and North Western and Union Pacific Railroads collaborated on the train named the *City of Los Angeles*. The *California Limited* and *Super Chief* trains ran along the middle route on the tracks of the Acheson, Topeka and Santa Fe. This route served the Route 66 communities between Albuquerque and Los Angeles. The *Golden State Limited* train

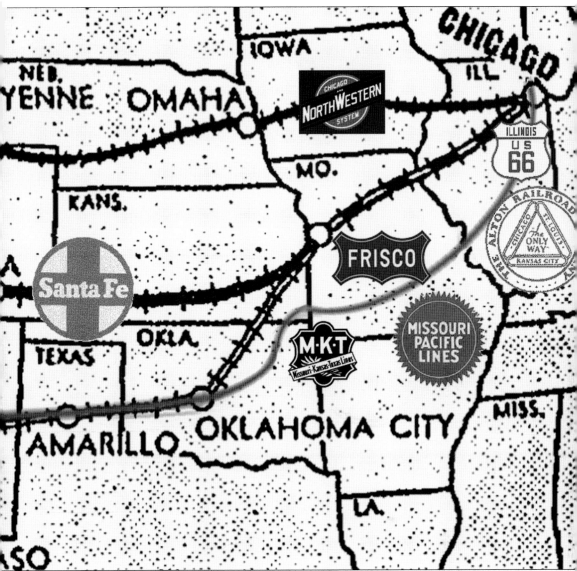

took the southern route, on the tracks of the Chicago, Rock Island and Pacific and the Southern Pacific, serving the 66 towns from Oklahoma City, Oklahoma, to Tucumcari, New Mexico. The Route 66 corridor, from Chicago to Oklahoma City, was served by various rail lines, including the Chicago and Alton; Missouri Pacific (MoPac); San Francisco and St. Louis (Frisco); and the Missouri, Kansas and Texas (Katy) Railroads. The gray line on the map indicates Route 66.

The illustration at left is from the May 1904 edition of a publication named *Out West*. The Acheson, Topeka and Santa Fe Railroad promised to whisk passengers between Los Angeles and Chicago on the *California Limited* train in 66 hours; this matched the transit time of the Union Pacific and Chicago, Rock Island and Pacific Railroads' *Golden State Limited* train. The 1918 illustration (below) from the *American Review of Reviews* shows the 23 trunk line railroads that used Chicago as a hub. It stated, "Chicago is a terminal city. No trains—either passenger or freight—run through it." People and cargo entering Chicago transferred to a different train if their destination was elsewhere. "Following the Galena and Chicago Union Railroad, which began operations in 1848, other railroads entered the field rapidly." By 1860, eight western and three eastern trunk lines had already started service terminating in Chicago.

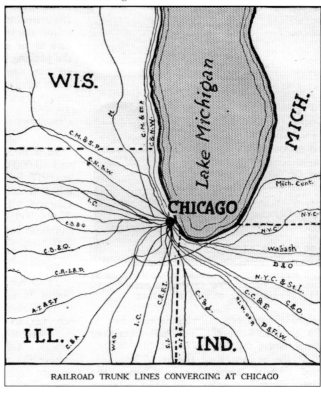

RAILROAD TRUNK LINES CONVERGING AT CHICAGO

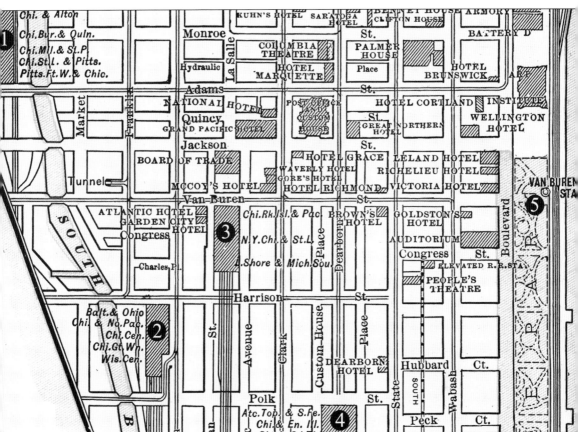

This *c.* 1893 map shows four of Chicago's six major rail terminals. The original Union Station (1) served five roads, including the Chicago and Alton and the Chicago, Burlington and Quincy Railroads. Grand Central Station (2) was home to the Baltimore and Ohio and Wisconsin Central Railroads. The Chicago, Rock Island and Pacific Railroad owned and operated the LaSalle Street Station (3), known as the Van Buren Station originally, in partnership with the Lake Shore and Michigan Southern Railroad. Dearborn (also known as Polk) Street Station (4) handled the passenger traffic for the Acheson, Topeka and Santa Fe, the Grand Trunk, and the Wabash Railroads. Van Buren Street Station (5) was a downtown commuter stop for the Illinois Central Railroad, whose main station was further south at Michigan Boulevard and Twelfth Street. The Chicago and North Western Railroad's station was west of downtown at Madison and Canal Streets. Arrayed on and around the future Route 66 corridor of Jackson Boulevard are over a dozen hotels serving the traveling public.

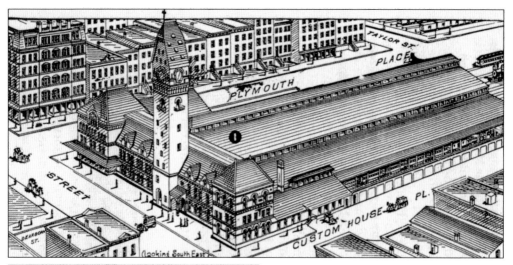

These illustrations from Rand McNally's 1893 *Bird's-Eye Views and Guide to Chicago* show Chicago's Dearborn Street (above) and LaSalle Street (5 in the image at left) Railroad Stations. The Dearborn Station, built in 1883, continued to serve the Acheson, Topeka and Santa Fe Railroad until Amtrak consolidated all Chicago passenger service at Union Station in the 1970s. The train sheds were demolished in 1976, and the building underwent conversion to offices and shops in the late 1980s. The Chicago, Rock Island and Pacific and Lake Shore and Michigan Southern Railroads built a station at LaSalle and Van Buren Streets in 1866 that was destroyed in the 1871 Chicago fire. According to the guide, "It was rebuilt in 1873, and its dedication in June of that year was made a civic musical festival. . . . Fifty-two Rock Island trains . . . arrive here daily, and 4,500 passengers arrive and depart daily" in 1893.

In 1903, the Chicago, Rock Island and Pacific and Lake Shore and Michigan Southern Railroads built their third terminal at LaSalle and Van Buren Streets (above). That same year, the Chicago, Rock Island and Pacific Railroad began their partnership with the Southern Pacific Railroad on the *Golden State Limited* train, which whisked passengers from Chicago to Los Angeles in 66 hours. The *Golden State Limited* train traveled by way of the eventual Route 66 corridor from Oklahoma City, Oklahoma, to Tucumcari, New Mexico. The LaSalle Street Station still serves suburban commuter trains, but a high-rise office building replaced the head house in 1982. The Illinois Central built the station shown below south of Grant Park at Michigan Boulevard and Twelfth Street in 1893. The tracks running north from the station towards the left edge of the postcard terminated at a rail yard on the south bank of the Chicago River.

Lake Front looking South, showing Logan Statue and Illinois Central Depot, Chicago.

The photograph above shows the Jackson Drive viaduct over the Illinois Central Railroad right-of-way, east of Michigan Boulevard. The staircase descending from the viaduct to the track platform leads to the Van Buren Street commuter rail station. The viaduct began serving Route 66 automobile traffic in 1937. In the photograph at left, electric commuter trains pass through Grant Park just south of Jackson Drive, with the Railway Exchange Building visible in the background. As noted in chapter 1, the Railway Exchange Building was home to the offices of the Chicago and Alton; the Chicago, Milwaukee and St. Paul; and the Acheson, Topeka and Santa Fe Railroads. The sign on the roof of the building was a 1950s addition, erected when the Santa Fe leased more than 50 percent of the exchange's office space. The exchange is now a protected Chicago Landmark as part of the Michigan Avenue Historic District.

The Chicago and North Western Railroad and its predecessor railways had four separate terminals on Kinzie Street between 1848 and 1911. The above postcard shows a bird's-eye view of the Chicago and North Western Railroad's fifth passenger terminal, which stood at Madison and Canal Streets west of downtown from 1911 to 1984. From here, travelers could take the *City of Los Angeles* train service to California. The station's architects, Charles Frost and Alfred Granger, also designed the Chicago and North Western Railroad's corporate office building (right). Located at the northeast corner of Jackson Boulevard and Franklin Street and completed in 1904, the building now contains the offices of the City Colleges of Chicago. Suburban commuter trains still use its rail right-of-way and train platforms, but an office and retail building replaced the terminal building in the mid-1980s.

Chicago's original Union Station (above) stood at the northeast corner of Adams and Canal Streets and served passengers from 1881 to 1923. In 1893, the station handled 251 arriving and departing trains daily, carrying 30,000 passengers. Railroads served by the station included the Chicago and Alton; the Chicago, Burlington and Quincy; the Chicago, Milwaukee and St. Paul; and the Pittsburg, Cincinnati, Chicago and St. Louis. Daniel Burnham's 1909 *Plan of Chicago* called for consolidating all of the city's rail service in a larger Union Station west of downtown, so the new 1924 station (below) had the capacity for 700 trains and 400,000 passengers per day. However the new station's tenants were the same that used old Union Station. Other railroads resisted civic pressure to relocate, citing their investment in their own facilities. Jackson Boulevard is the thoroughfare left of the station.

MAIN WAITING ROOM,
NEW UNION STATION,
CHICAGO

The new Union Station comprised two buildings located between Adams Street and Jackson Boulevard on either side of Canal Street. These two views show the interior of the west building's main waiting room. A postcard postmarked 1929 (above) shows the vaulted barrel-arched skylight, travertine marble walls, and Corinthian columns that contribute to the room's monumental scale. The view from the waiting room floor (below) shows the staircase leading up to the Canal Street doors near the south end of the station. These stairs figured prominently in the 1987 film *The Untouchables*, in which Andy Garcia shoots two mobsters while rescuing a baby in a carriage. Union Station is unique among large rail stations because it is configured with two stub-end terminals on its north and south sides as well as pass-through gates on its east end for trains that do not terminate at the station.

During World War II, passenger rail traffic increased, due in part to wartime gasoline rationing and curtailment of automobile manufacturing. The photograph at left shows the main ticketing concourse of Union Station's east building during the war years. The banner advertising war bonds hangs above the street-level doors leading to Canal Street, and below, the entry to a below-grade pedestrian walkway leads to the waiting rooms in the west building. The postcard below shows the station's Servicemen's Lounge, where armed service members could pass the time during stopovers between trains. Other amenities at the station included shops, restaurants, and a swimming pool. An office high-rise replaced the east station building in 1969. Currently Amtrak and suburban commuter rail trains use the station and its west building, which is Chicago's only terminal still standing and still in use for its original purpose.

THE SERVICEMEN'S LOUNGE, provided by Chicago Union Station Company, offers recreational, reading, writing and resting facilities for the benefit of men and women of the Armed Forces, at no charge to them. A specially built, large television screen features up-to-the-minute broadcasts of sports event, news happenings, pictures, etc. Travelers Aid Society hostesses are in constant attendance to assist strangers in Chicago with stopover time between trains.

Railroads using CHICAGO UNION STATION serve the entire United States: Pennsylvania Railroad to the east, northeast and southeast—Burlington Route and Milwaukee Road to the west and northwest —Gulf, Mobile & Ohio Railroad to the south and southwest. No matter where you live, a representative of one of these railroads is located in your vicinity, and will promptly answer your travel questions.

The Chicago, Burlington and Quincy Railroad built this 1911 building (above) on the block west of Union Station on Jackson Boulevard for its main offices. Designed by the architectural firm of Marshall and Fox, the building features an enameled cream-colored terra-cotta facade with delicate Gothic ornamentation. The postcard below is a souvenir of the Chicago, Burlington and Quincy Railroad's exhibit at the Century of Progress, Chicago's world's fair of 1933. Westbound trains out of Chicago included mail cars, on which the mail was sorted en-route by postal workers. After a series of mergers, the Chicago, Burlington and Quincy and the Acheson, Topeka and Santa Fe Railroads both became part of the Burlington Northern Railroad, which still operates freight service. One of their intermodal facilities, where cargo containers transfer from trains to trucks for local delivery, is located on Route 66 west of Chicago in Cicero.

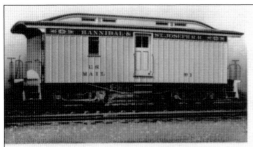

SEVENTY YEARS OF PROGRESS IN THE RAILWAY POST OFFICE

In a little car like this, on July 28, 1862, enroute from West Quincy to St. Joseph, Missouri over what is now a part of the Burlington main line from Chicago to Kansas City and St. Joseph, United States Mail was first sorted while in transit. The purpose was to speed the departure of the overland stage coach from St. Joseph to California.

At the right is the modern standard Railway Post Office, in several of which the California and other western mail is now sorted nightly on the Burlington fast mail trains between Chicago and Omaha.

The old and the new mail cars form a part of the Burlington Railroad exhibit at
A Century of Progress Exposition

As cars flooded Chicago's streets, safe rail crossings became a critical problem. Near the Chicago border with the town of Cicero, Ogden Avenue (Route 66) shared a four-lane subway under the Chicago, Burlington and Quincy Railroad with the traffic from two other streets. Each day, 31,000 vehicles squeezed into the passage, creating a near-constant bottleneck. According to the *Chicago Tribune*, the Illinois Division of Highways completed the viaduct in 1939, shown here, which they called their "most complicated grade separation problem ever tackled." The view above looks northeast toward Chicago; the view below shows an Ogden Avenue streetcar heading west into Cicero via a tunnel beneath the viaduct. The viaduct was a quarter-mile in length, and the roadway on the truss bridge was 45 feet above Cicero Avenue, the north–south cross street below. (Below, photograph by Truman Hefner, courtesy of the Krambles-Peterson Archive.)

Starting in the 1840s, railroads built their tracks approaching the city's periphery at grade level. As Chicago grew, the grid of city streets engulfed the tracks with no separation between urban neighborhoods and high-volume rail traffic. Five rail companies used the right-of-way across Ogden Avenue between Western Avenue and Rockwell Street, including the Chicago and North Western Railroad. A 700-foot-long viaduct carried Ogden Avenue over the tracks in 1892, but it was in severe disrepair by 1900, as shown in the *Chicago Tribune* illustration at right. In December 1900, a woman named Tillie Canniff fell through a hole in the wooden sidewalk to her death on the tracks below. The railroads made repairs, but by 1910, a new steel and concrete structure (below) elevated the tracks above grade.

As long-haul rail lines transported passengers to and from Chicago, rails of a different type assisted locals and visitors in navigating the city's streets. Horse-drawn street rail began on Ogden Avenue in the late 1870s and on Adams Street in 1885. The West Chicago Street Railroad Company started a cable car line in 1893 that ran on Adams Street downtown between Franklin and Dearborn Streets. At its peak, Chicago had the largest cable car system in the country. According to a souvenir booklet for the Chicago City Railway Company, the greatest difficulty faced by a street railway was clearing heavy winter snow. The illustration below shows a snow removal car for a Chicago cable line.

Chicago's first electric trolley began operation in 1893, but city ordinance prohibited overhead electric wires in the downtown area until 1905. This led to a hybrid system in which horse and electric cars came to the edges of downtown under their normal power, and then a cable car towed them around the loop circuit. The foreground of the postcard above shows a State Street cable car just north of Adams Street pulling a horsecar and a trolley car. The bottom photograph shows car No. 6053 crossing the Adams Street bridge into downtown on the Harrison-Adams line in August 1947. Adams Street trolley service ended in 1952 and was replaced by busses. Adams Street became westbound Route 66 in 1953. (Below, photograph by Thomas H. Desnoyers, courtesy of the Krambles-Peterson Archive.)

The postcard view above shows the Union Loop Elevated, a structure built in 1897 to bring rapid transit rail service into the downtown area without interfering with street traffic. In the bottom view, car No. 1784 heads westbound into Douglas Park on the Ogden-California line in 1950. The back of the highway shields for U.S. Routes 34 and 66 can be seen on the left of the image. The first half of the 20th century saw Chicago evolve from a reliance on rail to a reliance on automobiles. Transit service via elevated or subway took precedence over street rail, which was gradually eliminated by mid-century. The elimination of on-grade rail crossings through a program of viaduct building also continued the change in emphasis. The gateway of travel forged by water and expanded by rail became Route 66, the most famous of U.S. highways. (Below, photograph by Truman Hefner, courtesy of the Krambles-Peterson Archive.)

Four

SPREADING THE WEALTH

Prior to 1833, the only market for the agricultural products of the settlements along the Wabash River in southern Indiana was New Orleans. River pirates menaced the downriver trip on the Wabash, Ohio, and Mississippi Rivers, while highwaymen lurked along the tedious return journey on foot through sparsely settled regions.

The development of a market in Chicago gave the Wabash River farmers a choice, and by 1840, more of the goods of the Indiana settlers made their way overland to Chicago, 200 miles north, than to New Orleans. They drove their livestock on foot, and they hauled wheat, smoked ham, bacon, poultry, butter, lard, and other produce in Pennsylvania Conestoga wagons.

The Indiana Hoosier's wagons, drawn by eight yoke of oxen or six spans of horses, made their way up a trail known as the Vincennes Trace to an encampment along the lakefront in Chicago. As many as 160 wagons could be in the camp, from which the Hoosiers would sell or barter their wares. They would then load their prairie schooners with eastern goods shipped to Chicago on the Great Lakes and the Erie Canal. Salt, store goods, and stock for the village merchants would make their way back from Chicago and down the Vincennes Trace.

According to Milo M. Quaife's *Chicago's Highways Old and New* the Wabash valley wagons would disappear from Chicago once waterways and railroads created a conveyance choice with less cost and risk; as memorial to the days when Indiana farmers encamped on the lakefront, the city named the thoroughfare leading to the old campsite Wabash Avenue.

The Yankee merchants who settled Chicago would not have come if not for the Indiana farmers and others like them. This relationship created a metropolis whose rapid growth and wealth was unequaled in U.S. history; and the transportation network that grew from Chicago spread the wealth to the canal ports and rail stops along each route. Highways like Route 66 allowed any spot along the road to function as a port or stop, and any individual with a car and gas money could travel to Chicago to see the marketplace that created the American west.

As farmers brought their goods to market, there was always risk of loss. Chicago's developing transportation network allowed producers to transfer risk to operators of warehouses and grain elevators located along the transportation lines. Concerns over the prices paid by these intermediaries led the industry to create their own trade regulations; those who agreed to operate within these regulations joined to form the Chicago Board of Trade. Architect William Boyington designed the third home of the board, shown at left, built in 1885. It was one of the first financial institutions to locate on Jackson Street (the 1926 alignment of Route 66), where most buildings housed hotels, restaurants, and theaters. Structural instability in the board building's tower led to its removal in 1895. The 1925 postcard below looks south on LaSalle Street with the board building at the base of the T intersection with Jackson Boulevard.

By 1860, the Chicago Board of Trade had introduced a uniform system of grading grain by its quality. The board inspected all elevators and warehouses to insure the integrity of the grading process; since members of the board included both buyers and sellers, the result was one of the most respected and efficient commodities markets in the world. The 1912 postcard above shows the trading floor of the Chicago Board of Trade in the 1885 building. "An 1891 guidebook urged visitors to visit the public gallery at the Board of Trade . . . 'From this gallery a perfect view may be had of the operations on the floor,' it reported,'" accounted William Cronon in *Nature's Metropolis: Chicago and the Great West*. The 1958 postcard below shows the trading floor in the 1930 board building, built on the site of the 1885 building.

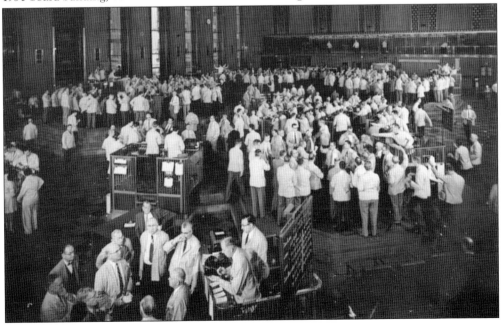

The postcard at left shows Jackson Boulevard looking east, with the 1885 Chicago Board of Trade building in the right foreground. The two statues located above the entrance now stand in a plaza next to the current board building (as shown on page 124). Beyond the board building is the 1886 Western Union Telegraph Building, which survived until 1957. The technology of the telegraph and telephone allowed corporations to remove their main offices from their industrial plants, leading to the innovation known as the downtown office building. The bottom postcard shows Jackson Boulevard looking east from the opposite side of the street. The Chicago Board of Trade is visible in the right foreground; from left foreground to background is the Royal Insurance building, the Illinois Trust and Savings Bank, the Grand Pacific Hotel, and the Federal Court House and Post Office.

Chicago's most interesting Streets: Jackson Blvd. from La Salle St. East.

The 1930 Chicago Board of Trade building, shown at right in a 1969 postcard view, was one of Chicago's tallest buildings when completed. The architectural firm of Holabird and Root designed the limestone-clad art deco masterpiece. A pyramidal roof with an aluminum statue of Ceres at the apex tops the 45-story, 612-foot-tall structure. John Storrs sculpted the statue of the Roman goddess of agriculture. The building's facade includes carvings such as the figures shown below. According to the *AIA Guide to Chicago*, artist Alvin Meyer designed the figures holding wheat and corn on either side of a central eagle and clock. With the 1885 and 1930 board buildings at its base on Jackson Boulevard, LaSalle Street became Chicago's financial center. Sometimes referred to as the Midwest's Wall Street, the thoroughfare was home to the city's largest banking, savings and loan, and insurance institutions.

From 1930 through 1955, Route 66 tourists going to the Chicago Board of Trade building could visit the trading floor gallery and ride the elevator up to the observatory near the top of the skyscraper. The postcard above shows the view east toward the lakefront. The tallest building in the view is the Straus Building discussed in chapter 1, located at the original starting point of Route 66. The photograph below shows the view east from the 30th floor of the 311 South Wacker building in 2005. Although the Chicago Board of Trade building dominates the view, the buildings in the distance are actually taller. Once the board's 25-year run as Chicago's tallest building ended, its observation deck closed. The board remains an important world financial exchange, and the art deco masterpiece is an enduring city landmark.

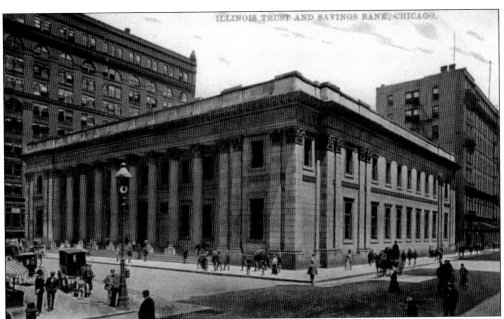

In 1896, the Grand Pacific Hotel's west half was demolished for the Illinois Trust and Savings Bank, seen looking northeast from the corner of Jackson Boulevard and LaSalle Street in the postcard view above. D. H. Burnham and Company designed the two-story bank building. According to the *Chicago Tribune*, in July 1919, a Goodyear Company dirigible crashed into the bank causing the death of 13 people. Within two weeks, the bank announced that they were merging with the Merchants Loan and Trust. By 1924, the Illinois Trust and Savings and Grand Pacific Hotel were razed; and the new Illinois Merchants Bank built a 19-story building on the north side of Jackson Boulevard between LaSalle and Clark Streets. The photograph below shows the building's LaSalle Street entrance, which illustrates a throwback to classicism in the building's design.

In 1928, the Illinois Merchants Bank merged again with the Continental National Bank and Trust to form the Continental Illinois Bank and Trust Company; the combined institution used the 1924 building on Jackson Boulevard between LaSalle and Clark Streets. The *Chicago Tribune* stated that the merger created "the first billion dollar banking institution for Chicago and . . . the second largest bank in the United States." The postcard view above shows the main banking lobby on the second floor. Facing the Continental Illinois bank on the west side of LaSalle Street is the 1922 Federal Reserve Bank, shown below. The architectural firm of Graham, Anderson, Probst and White designed both the Federal Reserve Bank and Continental Illinois Bank and Trust Company buildings. According to the *AIA Guide to Chicago*, Chicago's innovative architects despised the neoclassicism of the early 1920s; Louis Sullivan commented that since the Continental Illinois Bank and Trust Company re-created a Roman temple, the bankers should wear togas and speak Latin.

The Continental National Bank and Trust Company was located at the northeast corner of Clark and Adams Streets from 1907 to 1913 (right). While located here, it was the country's second largest national bank. In 1914, this building became the offices of the Commonwealth Edison Company. The January 10, 1912, *Chicago Tribune* stated, the Edison company "will occupy the ground floor . . . the street railroad systems of Chicago will also be in the building." The postcard below shows the Insurance Exchange, built in 1912 on Jackson Boulevard west of the Chicago Board of Trade from a design by D. H. Burnham and Company. The building's tenants included "fire and casualty insurance companies, insurance brokers, and other forms of business associated with underwriting" above a main floor of retail shops.

The 1912 building at the northeast corner of Jackson Boulevard and Jefferson Street (left) was designed by D. H. Burnham and Company as the offices and assembly plant of the Otis Elevator Company. Elisha Graves Otis invented the automatic elevator brake, which insured that an elevator car could not fall even if its hoist cable broke. Safe elevators meant that architects could design and build commercial buildings to new and greater heights. When the 16-story Monadnock Block (below) was built in 1891 at the southwest corner of Jackson Boulevard and Dearborn Street from a design by Daniel Burnham and John Root, it was briefly the tallest building in the world. It remains the tallest building anywhere supported by weight-bearing walls, which are 6 feet thick at street level. This austere building's unornamented facade tapers inward gracefully towards an outward curved roofline, resembling an Egyptian pylon.

MONADNOCK BLOCK, CHICAGO.

These photographs show the exterior and interior of the Rookery, built in 1888 at the southwest corner of LaSalle and Adams Streets from a design by Daniel Burnham and John Root. In contrast with the architects' sleek Monadnock Block, the Rookery's plentiful ornamentation and detail creates the look of a Moorish temple. The designer's own offices were on the top floor—in the early days of tall buildings, architects often moved into the top floors of their own designs to show their confidence in the safety of the structure. Frank Lloyd Wright remodeled the interior central atrium in 1907. The 600 offices in the building surround a central light and ventilation court. Tenants included brokers, private bankers, and financial agents. The Illinois Trust and Savings Bank was located here before moving on to their own building.

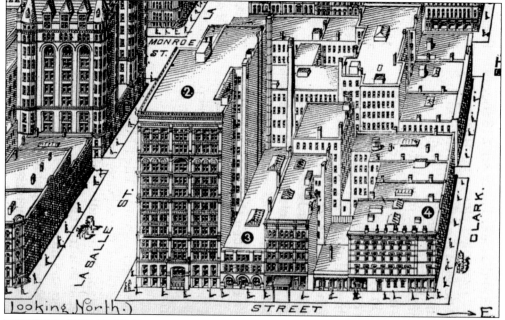

150—Field Building, Chicago

The drawing above, from Rand McNally's 1893 *Bird's-Eye Views and Guide to Chicago*, shows the view looking north on Adams Street between LaSalle and Clark Streets. William Le Baron Jenney designed the 1885 Home Insurance Building (2); it is widely considered to be the first building to use a metal skeleton method of construction with steel beams. Construction in 1931 of the Field Office Building (below) required demolition of all buildings on Adams Street between LaSalle and Clark Streets. The four corner sections of the building are 23 stories tall, and the central tower rises an additional 19 stories. Graham, Anderson, Probst and White designed the art deco building, marking a break from the classicism for which they were known. The Field Office Building was the last large downtown building completed in the 1930s; the Great Depression and World War II put new construction on hiatus.

The Field Office Building's LaSalle Street entrance (right) showcases the exterior's art deco details. Dark granite outlines the soaring entryway columns of carved limestone around huge plate glass windowpanes. The interior lobby (below) is a celebration of marble with metalwork of nickel, silver, and bronze. The lights projected upwards from wall sconces emphasizing the beige walls and white pilasters. A plaque near the LaSalle Street entrance commemorates the location of the Home Insurance Building and its importance to the evolution of skyscraper engineering. The lobby includes bank and retail shops; an additional floor of retail and restaurants is on the lower level. The Field Office Building is now the LaSalle National Bank Building, named for the building's largest tenant.

The home of Montgomery Ward and Company, built in 1899 at Madison Street and Michigan Avenue, was located a few blocks north of the eventual alignment of Route 66. The company revolutionized the mail-order business, taking advantage of Chicago's huge wholesale market and efficient rail network to ship orders across the country at prices normally lower than retail merchants could match. The building housed the mail-order operations and was open to visitors who could purchase from the catalog and have their goods shipped home. The 394-foot-tall tower was Chicago's highest point when built. The image below is from a souvenir booklet given to building visitors. The booklet stated, "After you have been our guest and seen all we have to offer, all we ask is that you tell your friends about it. We thrive under the searchlight."

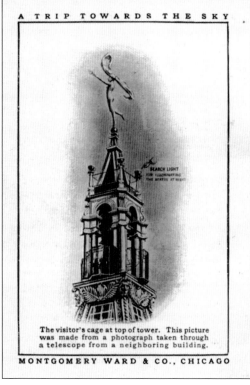

The visitor's cage at top of tower. This picture was made from a photograph taken through a telescope from a neighboring building.

Montgomery Ward and Company's hometown Chicago rival Sears, Roebuck and Company, relocated its merchandising operations into their own tower, completed in 1974 in the block bounded by Jackson Boulevard, Franklin Street, Adams Street, and Wacker Drive. The building's bottom 50 floors had 5,000 employees working on them. Each floor featured a massive 50,000 square feet of usable space. The tower allowed Sears, Roebuck and Company to consolidate operations from seven locations. The building currently retains the Sears name, although the company relocated in 1992. The 110-story building is the tallest in the United States. From 1887 to 1930, the southeast corner of Adams and Franklin Streets was the site of the Marshall Fields Wholesale Store, pictured below. H. H. Richardson, whose style was influential for younger architects including Louis Sullivan, designed the massive masonry structure. Many wholesalers and warehouses were located in the West Loop in the early 1900s.

The building above, located at the southwest corner of Adams and Green Streets, was converted to loft condominiums in 1998; previously it was one of three buildings used by Scotch Woolen Mills. The company manufactured suits made to custom measurements at prices below those charged for off-the-rack suits. Scotch Woolen Mills had agreements with independent stores across the U.S. and Canada. A customer could go to any agent store, get measured, and pick out a suit style and fabric. The store wired or phoned the order into the Chicago factory, which made the suit to order and shipped it the following day. The advertisement at left was part of the in-store display at the agent locations in 1926. Neighboring the Scotch Woolen Mills complex were light industries, clothing manufacturers, and wholesalers that supplied department stores and mail order houses.

In 1949, the Florsheim Shoe Company built their factory (above) at the northwest corner of Adams and Canal Streets, diagonally across the intersection from their previous location. The new factory won acclaim as one of the most efficient and modern manufacturing plants in the world. Like the rest of the apparel industry, Florsheim decided to open a new plant overseas in the 1990s to take advantage of cheaper labor; the building lives on after conversion to retail and residential loft condominiums. The Bays English Muffin Company has been producing muffins in Chicago since 1933, and has been in this location (right) on Jackson Boulevard between Morgan and Aberdeen Streets, since 1975. The company has announced no plans to relocate, although the former commercial and industrial properties surrounding it are undergoing retail and residential transformation at a speedy pace.

Revere Electric Company

DISTRIBUTORS OF

ELECTRICAL SUPPLIES

The Revere Electric Company was located on Jackson Boulevard between Halsted and Desplaines Streets from 1928 until the late 1950s. Their product catalog name, the *Messenger of Service,* was an attempt to tie the company's name to Paul Revere's service to the young United States with his legendary ride to deliver a message about the movement of British troops. This issue of the catalog (left) shows their Jackson Boulevard building as it looked in 1928. The catalog highlighted items manufactured directly by the company, such as service station and trolley car lighting, as well as many items for which they were the sole distributor. The photograph below shows an installation of their service station lighting. Construction of the Kennedy Expressway (Interstates 90 and 94) forced the Revere Electric Company to move to the northwest side of Chicago. It is now known as Revere-Holt after a merger.

The near–west side of Chicago was a hotbed of union organizing activity from the 1880s through the 1930s. The Haymarket Square incident of May 1886 occurred at Desplaines and Randolph Streets, when police marched into a union rally concerning the fight for a 40-hour workweek. During the ensuing confusion, a bomb exploded, killing one police officer immediately and mortally wounding six others. Many other strikes occurred, as workers organized to improve their economic and working conditions. The Route 66 corridor is still home to dozens of union locals, including the Painter's District Council Number 14 (above) at the corner of Adams and Laflin Streets. The art deco building is made of carved limestone and polished granite, which ironically require no paint. The sign below is on the grounds of the Teamster Union headquarters on Jackson Boulevard between Paulina Street and Ashland Avenue.

E. J. Lehman founded the Fair in 1875 in a small wooden building on State and Adams Streets. The store's name implied fair dealing for all customers and that the store was like a fair because it offered a wide variety of items for sale at cheap prices. In 1890, Lehman hired the firm of Jenney and Mundie to design a new building for the Fair, which filled the north side of Adams Street from State to Dearborn Streets. When completed in 1896, the Fair was the largest department store in the world. Its motto, "Everything for everybody, under one roof, at a lower price," created a model for department stores along Chicago's State Street and downtown shopping districts across the country. Montgomery Ward and Company purchased the Fair in 1964 for its downtown Chicago store, which remained open until it was razed in 1986.

Looking west from Michigan Avenue, the postcard at right from 1920 shows the elevated train tracks crossing Jackson Boulevard at the intersection with Wabash Avenue; at the northeast, northwest, and southwest corners is the 1916 Lyon and Healy, the 1910 Steger, and the 1917 Kimball buildings. All of these buildings featured showrooms for musical instrument manufacturers, as well as musical studios and sheet music retailers. When the Baldwin Piano Company moved to the southeast corner, the *Chicago Tribune* referred to this corner as the city's musical center. Lyon and Healy, founded in 1889, originally made many instruments including violins, pianos, mandolins, guitars, and organs. The postcard below shows Lyon and Healy's record room where customers could listen to Victor and Edison recordings before purchase. Still based in Chicago on Ogden Avenue, the company remains the world's most renowned manufacturer of harps.

275. Jackson Boulevard, Looking West, Chicago, Ill.

LYON & HEALY'S NEW VICTOR AND EDISON RECORD ROOM. YOU ARE WELCOME.   2745

1922. The force assembled at the Western Electric plant in Chicago.

A group of Western Electric men in 1881.

Some of the 37,000 workers in the world's telephone workshop

Western Electric

Since 1869 Makers of Electrical Equipment

On Ogden Avenue at Chicago's western border with Cicero, the Western Electric Hawthorne Works was the main manufacturer of the Bell Telephone System, where the inventions and innovations of Bell Labs became useful products. The plant produced the first vacuum tube in 1913 and the first desktop telephones in 1919. It later produced the first commercially successful movie sound system and was instrumental in creating air-to-ground communication methods. The facility covered five million square feet with 100 buildings and employed nearly 40,000 workers. This 1922 advertisement shows many of the employees of the Western Electric Hawthorne Works gathered to hear the company's chief executive address them by telephone from New York over public address equipment manufactured at the plant. The company remained in operation until the early 1980s; along with the financial institutions, wholesalers, warehouses, mail order companies, showrooms, and retail concerns gathered along the corridor of Route 66, the Western Electric Hawthorne Works was a part of the conversation of commerce that took place between Chicago and its transportation hinterland. Where commerce spread, travelers would roam.

Five

SERVING THE TRAVELER

When roads are built, opportunities develop for entrepreneurs with an idea and a desire. Travelers far from home in need of food, lodging, service, and local transport are willing to pay a fair price for services rendered. This is true whether the road traveled is made of iron rails or concrete slabs.

Franklin Parmelee lived in the Grand Pacific Hotel on Jackson Boulevard in Chicago. Just west on Jackson Boulevard, his company's stables cared for their lifeblood—their horses. Parmelee had left his home in upstate New York at age 12 for work as a stagecoach relay boy, and then as a driver. He was an entrepreneur who saw an opportunity in the fact that passengers whose rail travel did not terminate in Chicago needed assistance to transfer as much as three miles to change depots and trains. According to David M. Young's *Chicago Transit*, Parmelee bought out the omnibus service of several hotels to start his own depot transfer line. On May 9, 1853, he went into business with 30 horses, 12 hired hands, and six wagons.

In time, Parmelee had agreements with all of the railways terminating in Chicago so that a through ticket would include a transfer of travelers and their baggage between stations on his omnibuses. Later the Parmelee Company transitioned to motor coaches and busses and continued in operation long after Parmelee's death. According to David M. Young's *The Iron Horse and the Windy City*, the company lives on as the Continental Air Transport Company, hauling passengers in vans from downtown hotels to Chicago's airports.

Chicago had many entrepreneurs with a Parmelee mind-set who seized opportunity by serving the city's transient population. Hoteliers such as John Drake and Zora Vidas; restaurateurs including Albert Pixley and William Ehlers, William and Lou Mitchell, and John Raklios; and automobile sales and service businesses with names such as Geller, Buresch, and Warshawsky all served the Chicago Route 66 corridor in the rail and automobile eras.

Franklin Parmelee's business began with second-hand stagecoaches bought from over-the-road operators put out of work by the railroads. In addition to depot transfer, Parmelee started regular commuter omnibus service in 1855 along State Street and started the city's first street railway. According to David M. Young's *Chicago Transit*, during the Civil War, he sold his outside interests to concentrate upon the railway transfer business. The photograph above shows Parmelee motor coaches parked outside of Union Station in 1925. Old Union Station is still standing in the background, with the new 1924 station shown on the right. The advertisement at right appeared in a 1920 flier for a Chicago tour company. Young's book *Iron Horse* states that by 1930, Morris Markin, who was involved with the Checker Cab Manufacturing Company, owned the Parmelee Transportation Company. (Above, photograph by A. W. Johnson, courtesy of the Krambles-Peterson Archive.)

Parmelee was a permanent resident of the Grand Pacific Hotel, shown above as it looked from 1872 until 1895. The Lake Shore and Michigan Southern and Chicago, Rock Island and Pacific Railroads owned the hotel, which was located on Jackson Boulevard between LaSalle and Clark Streets. John Drake leased and operated the hotel from 1874 to 1894, and under his management, the Grand Pacific Hotel gained a reputation for being Chicago's finest hotel. The Republican party and the nation's railroad executives regularly held meetings and conventions here. In 1895, a dispute among the property's owners led to the demolition of the western half of the hotel. A remodeled and modernized Grand Pacific Hotel opened on the east end of the property in 1898, as shown in the postcard below. Drake died in 1895; his sons later operated the Drake and Blackstone Hotels on Michigan Boulevard.

101 Great Northern Hotel and
Office Building,
Chicago, Ill.

The Great Northern Hotel was located at
the northeast corner of Jackson Boulevard
and Dearborn Street. Designed by Burnham
and Root, the hotel opened in 1892 with
500 guest rooms and eight dining rooms.
A 1930s remodeling resulted in a reduction
to 400 guest rooms with private baths. The
Great Northern Coffee Shop served meals for
35–85¢, and in the Fountain Luncheon dinner
was $1. Single rooms were $2.50 per night,
and double rooms were $3.50. The hotel's
brochures boasted that they offered "The most
comfortable and pleasant dining rooms in
Chicago—*air-conditioned*—with temperature
never exceeding seventy degrees. . . . It
is because of this convenience, service,
reasonable rates, comfort and cuisine that
the 'Travel-Wise' select the Great Northern
Hotel." The Dirksen Federal Center, built in
1964, now occupies the site of the
Great Northern Hotel.

The buildings in the 1959 postcard view at right were originally the Hotel Kaiserhof, until anti-German sentiment before World War I led the owners to change the name to the Hotel Atlantic. The original eight-story building on the left dates from 1892, and Marshall and Fox designed the 18-story addition on the right, constructed in 1915. The hotel was located on Clark Street south of Jackson Boulevard. The postcard below shows the Atlantic Hotel's lobby. A room in the 1930s was $2 per night or $2.50 with a private bath. The October 3, 1965, *Chicago Tribune* noted the same family ran the historic hotel since 1903. The newspaper's restaurant reviewer Kay Loring commented on the excellent German dishes served for lunch in the Old World Dining Room, and for dinner in the more modern Clipper Room.

A Chicago social organization named the Midland Club built the combination club and office tower (left) in 1928. The organization hoped the office tower leases would pay the construction bonds and property taxes, but the Great Depression left rentable office space vacant. The club leased three floors of their space in 1935 as a hotel, and then sold the building in the 1940s to pay off back taxes. The Midland Hotel expanded into the entire space once taken by the club and became famous for reasonable prices and friendly service. Locals and visitors enjoyed the Midland's two restaurants: the Ticker Tape, an art deco steak and seafood eatery; and the Exchange, an intimate space on the balcony overlooking the lobby. The Midland survived until the 1990s when most other old downtown hotels closed; the building is now home to a W Hotel.

MIDLAND
HOTEL

"Chicago's
Friendliest"

172 W. ADAMS ST.
CHICAGO 3, ILL.

Many hotels in Chicago catered to permanent residents as well as visitors. In their prime, establishments like the Rosemoor Hotel (above), located on Jackson Boulevard west of Ashland Avenue, catered to young men new to the city and to traveling salesmen. Today the Rosemoor Hotel provides housing for low-income residents; the bellhop on the sign is a vestige of a very different era. The 1930 postcard below shows the lobby of the Hotel Vernon, which was on Jackson Boulevard east of Halsted Street. Billing itself as an "Exclusive Residential Hotel," it also provided short-term stays for Chicago visitors or long-term rooms mainly for single males. Torn down in the 1980s, the Vernon's former location is now a parking lot.

LOUNGE, HOTEL VERNON, 758 JACKSON BLVD., CHICAGO

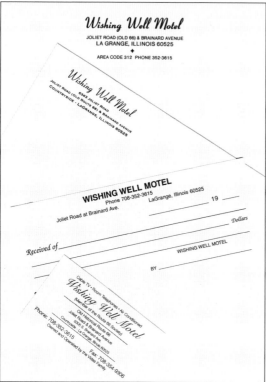

The postcard above and the stationery, receipt, and business card at left are from the Wishing Well Motel, located 15 miles west of Chicago on Route 66. Charles Vidas and his son, Emil, purchased the motel in 1958 when it was 17 years old. They connected the 10 separate cottages and built eight new units. Emil and his wife, Zora, ran the Wishing Well Motel together when their recurrent visitors included members of big bands, who frequently played at nearby suburban supper clubs. The motel appealed to Chicago visitors who enjoyed the clean, inexpensive rooms and short drive into the city. Travelers from the east would also use the Wishing Well Motel on their way west for their "California Trip." Zora ran the motel herself after Emil died in 1987; upon Zora's death in 2005, the motel closed its doors.

From the 1900s through the 1930s, John Raklios was Chicago's Café King, with over 20 locations in Chicago boasting courtesy, well-prepared food, service, and cleanliness. In 1919, Raklios wrote of his business in *American Restaurant* that he equipped his "places with an arrangement for seating and service capable of competing with the most expensive cafes together with complete menus." At the dawn of the automobile era, Raklios and his wife, Mary, created the standard for Chicago's low-priced eateries. Four of the chain's restaurants were located on the original alignment of Route 66 and all were within two miles of the route. The Raklios chain was unable to survive the Great Depression, but the attention to good food and service at affordable prices is the legacy of the restaurants that still exist both in Chicago and along all of Route 66.

Fred Harvey gained fame by operating the dining cars of the Acheson, Topeka and Santa Fe Railroad. He expanded his relationship with the Santa Fe Railroad by opening Harvey House restaurants and hotels in the cities served by the railroad from Chicago to Los Angeles. When the new Union Station opened in 1925, the Harvey Company supplied all concessions in the complex, including seven restaurants, stores, and shops. Hungry travelers also had the option of eating at the Pixley and Ehlers cafeteria at the southwest corner of Route 66 and Canal Street south of the station. The cafeteria chain had started in Chicago in 1899 and boasted they were "the place to please your palate and balance your budget." Pixley and Ehlers were 24-hour eateries with 15 locations in the city, famous for their "American Pie." The postcard below shows one of their interiors from about 1933.

A Typical PIXLEY AND EHLERS RESTAURANT at 68 E. Lake Street -- CHICAGO

In 1923, Lou Mitchell's father, William, opened an eatery on Jackson Boulevard in Chicago. The stock market crash of 1929 and the ensuing Great Depression caused other restaurateurs to close, leaving William Mitchell to absorb the clientele. Mitchell called in his children to help. Lou, Polly, and Demi Mitchell came in and served the customers, and Mitchell concentrated on the kitchen. Today the restaurant survives on the same block, under the founder's son's name, and Route 66 travelers flock to this now-traditional starting point of the journey west. "Everything we serve is fresh, never frozen, the best quality, [including] eggs, meats, real mashed potatoes, fresh-squeezed orange juice," says Heleen Thanas, Lou Mitchell's modern-day manager. Trends come and go, but Lou Mitchell's has stuck to their original formula for success. The restaurant is located on Jackson Boulevard, one block west of Union Station.

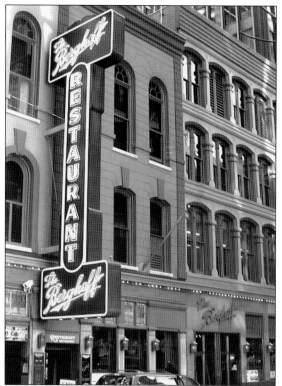

The Berghoff opened in Chicago at State and Adams Streets in 1898 as a saloon that offered free sandwiches for lunch with the purchase of a nickel beer. During Prohibition, the Berghoff moved east a few doors to its present location and changed its emphasis to quality German American cuisine served for moderate prices. In 1933, Herman Berghoff was issued Chicago Liquor License No. 1 on the day Prohibition was repealed. Visitors have flocked to this city institution for the Dortmunder-style beer, 14-year-old private-label bourbon, hand-carved roast beef sandwiches, Weiner schnitzel, sauerbraten, creamed spinach, and apple strudel. The buildings that house the Berghoff are some of the oldest in Chicago's Loop, built within a year after the Chicago fire of 1871. The 1998 menu below celebrated the restaurant's 100th anniversary with images from their history. In 2006, Herman Berghoff's great-granddaughter took over the restaurant.

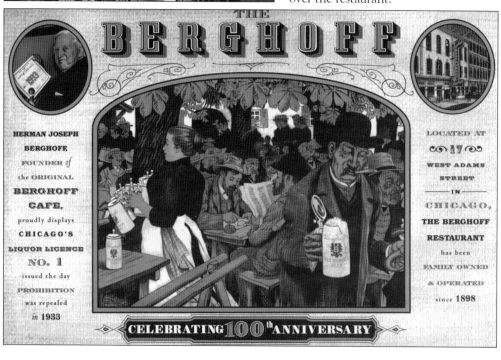

In 1950, brothers Jimmie, Nick, Peter, and Vannie Gallios purchased Miller's Pub, a Chicago landmark on Adams Street west of Wabash Avenue. The pub had been in business since 1935, but had fallen on hard times until revitalized by the work ethic of the Gallios family. During the 24-year span that Adams Street served westbound Route 66 travelers, Miller's Pub was a favorite downtown eating-place for locals, visitors, and celebrities. Signed photographs of famous patrons, such as Jimmy Durante, Frank Sinatra, and Tony Bennett, cover the walls. In 1989, Miller's Pub was forced to move when their building was demolished. They moved to 134 South Wabash (above), a few steps north of Adams Street, where they continue to thrive. The Wabash location was formally Lander's Restaurant, as seen in the 1953 postcard below.

Cafe Bohemia "Famous Dinners"

Eight Course Dinner

★ **FOR GOURMET OF WILD GAME**

Broiled Northern Moose Steak	6.9
Broiled Elk Steak with Wild Rice	6.9
Broiled Western Buffalo Steak with Wild Rice	6.9
Broiled "Our Famous" Buffalo-Burger, French Fried Onions	4.7
Broiled Venison Steak or Chops with Wild Rice	6.9
Broiled Bear Steak or Chops with Wild Rice	6.9
Broiled Western Mountain Sheep, with Wild Rice	6.9
Broiled Western Antelope Steak or Chops, Wild Rice	6.9
Roast Native Beaver, Wild Rice (3 hour notice)	6.9
Braised Steak Strips of African Lion-Grand Marnier Sauce	7.9
Sauted Steak Strips of Bengal Tiger, Wild Rice	7.9
Roast ½ Mallard Duck Under Glass, Wild Rice (3 hour notice)	6.9
Roast ½ Pheasant Under Glass with Wild Rice (3 hour notice)	6.9
Roast Whole Game Cornish Hen with Wild Rice (1 hour notice)	5.9
Cafe Bohemia Northern Venison Stew, Silver Casserole	4.9

Café Bohemia stood at the northwest corner of Adams and Clinton Streets from 1936 to 1986. Joe Basek, an avid hunter who introduced wild game to the menu, started the restaurant, later run by his stepson James Janek Jr. The restaurant also served Czech cuisine and sauces. Janek was famous for his forecast of winter weather, based on the amount of fat he found stored around the bear meat he served. The menu above shows some of the more exotic fare served by the café, including beaver, African lion, and Bengal tiger. The restaurant also boasted that they were the first to serve Buffalo Burgers, made from lean ground American bison meat. After Café Bohemia closed, its building was home to several restaurants including Ranalli's Pizza, below, before the building's removal for an office tower in 2004.

Chicago's original Greek enclave, the Greek Delta, was south of Route 66 in the triangular area bounded by Halsted Street, Polk Street, and Blue Island Avenue. When the city built the University of Illinois at Chicago campus on the Greek Delta site in the 1960s, many Greek business owners purchased property just north of the old district; Chicago's new Greektown was born. Previously Greek restaurateurs featured mainly American fare; but when the Parthenon opened south of Jackson on Halsted Street in 1969, they pioneered in promoting traditional Greek dishes to the public. Greek Islands opened in 1971 on Jackson east of Halsted Street, and later moved to the southwest corner of Adams and Halsted Streets. Rodity's came along in 1973. Chicago's Greektown served America's first Gyros sandwich, and it was where the traditional cheese dish Saganaki was first served flambéed at table side.

One of the Chicago area's best examples of a car culture-era drive-in restaurant is still thriving at 6031 West Ogden Avenue in Cicero, as seen above. When it opened in the 1950s, Henry's was a small food stand with a walk-up window and no indoor seating. The slogan, "It's a Meal in Itself," refers to the classic way of serving Chicago-style hot dogs in the same bag with French fries and pickle spear. The Henry's menu is extensive and their clientele faithful. Snuffy's 24 Hour Grill (below) on Joliet Road west of Riverside Drive in McCook is a perfect highway eatery, and little has changed from its 1964 opening. Booths with vinyl-covered seating and walnut-grain Formica tabletops line the east wall, with classic diner-style stools at the counter along the west wall. The fare is typical diner food made well.

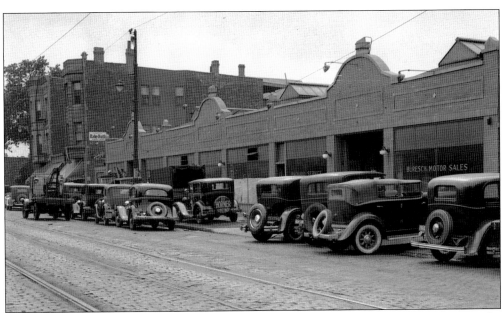

Ogden Avenue became a state highway in 1919, and by the start of Route 66 in 1927, the Chicago city directory listed 14 filling stations, eight automobile supply and towing companies, and a half-dozen automobile sales concerns along the thoroughfare. The 1933 photograph above shows the service department of Buresch Motor Sales, a Packard dealership, which was located at 4038 West Ogden Avenue. Other brands of automobiles available along Ogden Avenue included nearly forgotten nameplates such as Gray-Dort and the familiar rolling stock sold at Emil Denemark Cadillac. Ben Geller Chevrolet was located at 3651 West Ogden Avenue from at least 1957, when its first advertisement appeared in the *Chicago Tribune*, until 1979. Ben Geller Chevrolet billed itself as "Chicago's Fastest Growing Dealer" on the back of the early-1960s postcard, seen below.

In 1915, Israel Warshawsky pioneered the used automobile parts business at his first location on Chicago's south side. Originally a wholesaler of rebuilt parts for the car service industry, Warshawsky opened retail outlets such as the one above at 3924 Ogden Avenue to sell through to the car enthusiasts who repaired their own vehicles. The advertisement below from the 1930 Chicago Red Book indicates that Warshawsky's business had grown to the point that they could claim to be the "World's Largest Auto Replacement Parts House." In 1934, Warshawsky's son Roy started the mail-order catalog, J. C. Whitney, which is known to motor heads everywhere.

The proprietor of Joe's Auto and Cycle Supply, Joe Steinlauf, mailed the postcard at right in 1948 to a woman in Wisconsin to whom he was offering $5 for a used bicycle. Steinlauf opened his business in 1919; today a Lawndale Christian Health Center clinic occupies his old building. Unlike Ogden Avenue in Chicago, Route 66 through Berwyn remains a center of car culture, with automobile dealerships and supply businesses, gas stations, and car washes. Ogden Top and Trim (below) located in Berwyn at 6609 West Ogden Avenue, specialized in carriage harnesses and buggy whips when they opened in 1919. Still owned and operated by the family of the founder, they now restore historic automobile interiors, and they do custom fabric and cushion work in addition to automotive body repair and painting.

The 1963 photograph above shows U.S. Routes 34 and 66 shields on Adams Street, looking west at Desplaines Street. The location of the Super Car Wash and Sinclair Service Station is now a parking lot. The photograph below shows a typical 1970s Standard Oil gas station, located at Adams Street and Ogden Avenue in Chicago. The image shows the view looking northeast on Ogden Avenue on December 24, 1976, one month before the final Route 66 signs were removed in Illinois. Both of these automobile service businesses are now gone, as the former Route 66 corridor's through traffic was siphoned to the interstates. (Above, photograph by Perry E. Borchers, courtesy of the Library of Congress, Prints and Photographs Division; below, photograph by Art Peterson, courtesy of the Krambles-Peterson Archive.)

Six

SURVIVING
THE INTERSTATES

From 1919 to 1931, Frank T. Sheets served the Illinois Division of Highways as superintendent and chief highway engineer. During his tenure with the division, the state of Illinois developed from a state stuck in the mud to the number one state in the union in terms of the mileage of paved highways. He served a term as president of the American Association of State Highway Officials and was on the executive committee that approved the original alignment of Route 66.

After leaving public service, Sheets became the consulting engineer and director of development for the Portland Cement Association. On April 14, 1937, he delivered an address titled "The Highway of Tomorrow," which was prescient in realizing future problems. He stated that "tomorrow's highway system" would have various structures to serve different needs. Terminal facilities, "elevated or depressed limited ways" would be built "at the edge of . . . congested areas" to collect traffic from and to the urban area. Main superhighways would carry traffic for "transcontinental and intersectional travel." These highways would have four to eight traffic lanes, with no grade crossings. "These highways will avoid all cities and towns."

Main trunk highways would feed traffic to superhighways, would serve "other inter-city, inter-state and inter-sectional traffic," and would avoid "built-up sections of cities and towns." Bypasses keeping traffic "out of congested urban centers" would offer "the most reasonable insurance of convenience, peace of mind and efficiency in conducting normal business and social affairs within those communities." In all cases, Sheets advocated improved roads to best assist existing populations. Massive new superhighways were to go around urban populations, not through them.

Unfortunately the largest city in Sheets's home state was not listening. By 1940, planners had decided upon a network of radial superhighways penetrating directly to Chicago's center. The Eisenhower Expressway tore a swath one-quarter mile wide through established communities, and the Stevenson Expressway finished the job of siphoning through-traffic away from the Route 66 corridor. Decades of decay followed; businesses with luck and resolve persevered. Others now hope the Route 66 heritage will help meet their communities' future challenges.

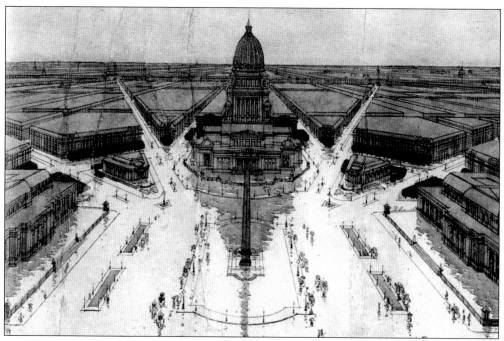

Daniel Burnham's 1909 *Plan of Chicago* envisioned a civic center west of the Chicago River at Halsted and Congress Streets, as shown above. Radiating from the civic center would be a network of grand boulevards; Congress Parkway was the "Axis of Chicago," and according to the *Chicago Tribune*, "a plaisance of carriageways, plazas, monuments, and landscaping." The drawing at left shows the pentagonal civic center with Congress Parkway running vertically at the center (west is at the top). When Burnham published the *Plan of Chicago*, land around Congress Parkway assumed speculative value. Housing stock in that corridor was mainly multiple-family rental property. Landowners assumed they would sell their property profitably when needed for the coming improvements, so many spent the bare minimum on maintenance. The economic demographics of the corridor shifted downward as the neglected structures deteriorated.

Burnham published the *Plan of Chicago* the same year that Ford introduced the Model T; the *Plan of Chicago* could not envision that an automobile superhighway would decrease property values and negatively influence the community's livability. By 1929, after Route 66 was already established, Burnham's associate Edward Bennett revived the Congress Superhighway plans. His concept called for a highway with separate directional lanes and a complete grade separation from surface streets. The claim was that well-planned landscaping would help support abutting realty value. After delays due to the Great Depression and World War II, work on the Congress (soon renamed Eisenhower) Expressway finally began in the 1950s. This photograph shows the spaghetti-bowl interchange built at the confluence of the Kennedy, Dan Ryan, and Eisenhower Expressways at Halsted and Congress Streets, where Burnham once envisioned a grand civic center.

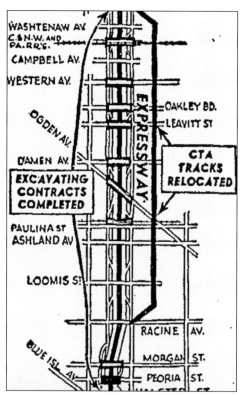

The R. L. Polk 1928–1929 *Chicago Numerical Street and Avenue Directory* listed 35 businesses and 47 residential units on Ogden Avenue between Paulina Street and Damen Avenue. The three-block stretch of Route 66, located near the Illinois Medical District, contained 11 medical supply concerns. Nurses' uniforms were available from Anna Welch at 1909 Ogden Avenue, and from Jane and Anna Welch at 1910 Ogden Avenue. Joseph LaGrasse at 1937 Ogden Avenue and George Harris at 1835½ Ogden Avenue operated barbershops, and Mayer Davis's tailor shop at 1914 Ogden Avenue provided custom alterations. The stretch included three restaurants, two printers, a jeweler, a grocer, a florist, and a drug store. The October 5, 1953, *Chicago Tribune* graphic at left shows completed excavating contracts in a portion of the Congress Expressway project that included the Ogden Avenue crossing. The photograph below shows the Ogden Avenue viaduct as it looks today. The old neighborhood has been long forgotten.

By 1960, transportation officials advised motorists using Route 66 to jog north on the Tri-State tollway and use the new Congress Expressway rather than follow Route 66 into Chicago. Completion of the Southwest Expressway (Interstate 55) east of the Tri-State tollway was four years away, but already through-traffic was encouraged to avoid the corridor of Ogden Avenue, Jackson Boulevard, and Adams Street. The 1960 *Chicago Tribune* illustration above shows the proposed route of the Southwest Expressway and the recommended bypass. Also in 1960, viaducts for Jackson Boulevard and Adams Street opened across the excavated Northwest (now Kennedy) Expressway corridor. Businesses displaced by this project included the Revere Electric Company (discussed on page 86), the Mountain Valley Spring Water Company, and the Upson-Walton Rope Company. The photograph below shows the Kennedy Expressway with the Jackson Boulevard viaduct in the background, as seen from the Adams Street viaduct in 2000.

Road to Follow Old Canal

The July 1960 *Cook County Highways* noted that the "I and M Canal was once an enterprise of wide importance." The Illinois and Michigan Canal opening "brought a revolution in travel and commerce." The canal's "bed is to become a modern expressway." The article discussed the marvelous historic value of the canal that they were bulldozing. The October 9, 1961, *Chicago Tribune* graphic above shows the planned route of the Southwest Expressway through the canal corridor. In the image below, a guardrail and limestone embankment is all that remains from the Lawndale Avenue bridge near Summit. The bridge over the Sanitary and Ship Canal carried traffic for Illinois State Route 4 (Route 66's precursor) prior to 1927. Construction of the Interstate 55 interchange with Illinois State Route 171 eliminated the connecting section of roadway, so the Lawndale Avenue bridge became a bridge to nowhere and was later removed.

The Southwest (Stevenson) Expressway opened in 1964, but Route 66 within Chicago remained on Ogden Avenue, Jackson Boulevard, and Adams Street. As work on Interstate 55 through Illinois continued and new sections of the limited access expressway opened, markers identified the new highway as both Interstate 55 and Route 66. In 1976, the Illinois Department of Transportation decided that both route numbers were no longer required, so Route 66 was decommissioned. The photograph on the right shows workers John Chesniak (left) and Gus Schultz taking down the final signs from a utility pole on Jackson Drive near Lake Shore Drive on January 17, 1977. The signs of negative impact on the old highway corridor underscore the importance of through traffic in the effected communities. In the image below, a ghost sign is all that remains of a service station at the northwest corner of Adams and Green Streets.

GAS VILLAGE

OGDEN
&
HAMLIN

- 24 Hour Towing
- Comp. Auto Repair
- Major & Minor
  Tune-Ups
- Tires - Batteries
- Accessories
- Trailer Renting

3801 W Ogden   762-7694

In 1925, Louis Ehrenberger purchased the lot at 3801 West Ogden Avenue next to his home in Chicago's North Lawndale neighborhood and built a filling station. John J. Murphy operated the station and later purchased it from Ehrenberger. The Murphy station sold Standard gasoline through the mid-1960s, staying in business under the same ownership for 40 years. Yellow Pages listings show a name change to S&B Standard Service in 1970. The 1971 advertisement above for Gas Village indicates that the business changed hands again, but it continued to operate through most of the Route 66 era. After removal of the gasoline tanks from the property, the building saw use as a car wash and automobile repair business. Today the Castle Car Wash stands empty and abandoned, as shown below, a relic from a different era with an uncertain future.

The photograph above shows the building at 4038 West Ogden Avenue that formerly housed Buresch Motor Sales (discussed on page 107). Like many other former automotive service buildings along old Route 66 in the North Lawndale neighborhood, this building stands unused and empty. The three-story building in the center of the photograph below was the location of Joe's Auto and Cycle Supply (discussed on page 109). Apparently a family member continued to operate a business in Joe's Auto and Cycle Supply's old location, evidenced by the ghost sign on the side of the building that identifies the concern as the "Fred Steinlauf Safety Center." The building is now in use as part of the non-profit Lawndale Christian Health Center.

The vacant lot above is the site of Ben Geller Chevrolet (discussed on page 107). The dealership suffered a setback in 1979 when heavy snow on the roof caused a collapse; the owners closed the business rather than trying to rebuild and persevere. A Sinclair filling station stood at 2363 West Ogden Avenue from at least 1928. The photograph below shows the former Sinclair filling station as it looked in 2006. The Route 66 corridor in the North Lawndale neighborhood has many vacant lots and buildings, stark evidence of the neighborhood's six decades of economic distress. The Historic Chicago Greystone Initiative, launched in 2006, created a mechanism to restore North Lawndale's housing stock but, so far, there is no program to preserve the commercial structures on Route 66.

The photograph above shows the Western Electric Hawthorne Works on Ogden Avenue at the Chicago-Cicero border. In the photograph on the right, an industrial building at 4401 West Ogden Avenue has signs left over from its previous use by Core Automotive Suppliers, a rebuilder of used car parts. Both buildings still enjoy partial use by concerns much smaller than the original occupants. The economics behind the closing of Western Electric Hawthorne Works and the reduction of industrial business on Chicago's West Side go far beyond the redirection of street traffic to the interstates, but the results further encumber the Route 66 corridor with a challenge requiring massive reuse, restoration, and hopefully at least some preservation. The improvement of the North Lawndale neighborhood's residential property puts unprotected commercial structures in greater danger, as developers could raze vacant or underused buildings on Ogden Avenue in favor of redevelopment.

The photograph above shows the McCook stone quarry north of Route 66. Quarrying in the McCook area began in the 1880s, and in 1976, Vulcan Materials Corporation expanded quarrying to most property on either side of Route 66 between Fifty-fifth Street and East Avenue. In 1998, the Illinois Department of Transportation closed Route 66 through Vulcan Materials Corporation's quarries. Then-mayor of McCook Patrick Gorski stated that "the road basically split in half and was actually moving, therefore causing certain sections of the roadway to sink . . . crack, and . . . explode from the pressure. . . . Limestone in the area was mined right up to about fifteen feet . . . of the Historic Highway 66 corridor." In 2001, the *Chicago Tribune* stated that "Vulcan blames Mother Nature . . . the rock cracks extend 400 feet down . . . farther than Vulcan has ever mined." A lawsuit remains pending between Illinois Department of Transportation and Vulcan Materials Corporation and the road remains closed, as seen below.

The photograph above shows two greystones on Avers Street near Ogden Avenue in the North Lawndale neighborhood. Developer Jan Kralovec built multi-family homes along Avers Street from 1892 through 1894 in anticipation of new streetcar service in the area. Restoration of homes along three blocks of Avers Street began in the 1990s, an early impetus for the current Historic Chicago Greystone Initiative. In 2005, the village of Lyons completed their landscaped Riverwalk along the Des Plaines River, as seen at right. The brick-paved path, located north of the original alignment of Route 66, begins near the base of the landmark Hofmann Tower, then meanders west along the wooded south bank of the Des Plaines River. The 1908 Hofmann Tower houses the exhibits of the Lyons Historical Museum. The castellated tower is an early example of reinforced concrete construction; its facade is severely delaminated and still in need of restoration.

The 1914, Cook County Hospital (above) was located south of Route 66 at 1835 West Harrison Street. From the 1920s through the 1950s, it was the world's largest medical institution, nicknamed "Chicago's Statue of Liberty" since it served the needs of many indigent immigrants. Current plans call for the building to undergo exterior restoration and commercial redevelopment. Originally the two statues shown below stood above the entrance to the 1885 Chicago Board of Trade building. They now stand in a plaza west of the current Chicago Board of Trade building. DuPage County Forest Preserve workers found the statues near Downers Grove on property formerly owned by an early-1900s Chicago Board of Trade speculator who seems to have taken the marble figures when the old building was demolished in 1929. The statues, symbolizing industry and agriculture, were returned to Jackson Boulevard and Route 66 in 2005.

Since Route 66 ceased existence as an official highway, enthusiasts have worked to preserve the route and its icons. The Route 66 Association of Illinois was formed in 1989; the association sponsors preservation projects and runs the Route 66 Hall of Fame Museum in Pontiac. In 1995, the Illinois Department of Transportation placed historic route markers along most of old Route 66 in Illinois, including the sign shown here located on Adams Street west of Michigan. Since 1999, the National Park Service's Route 66 Corridor Preservation Program has provided cost-share grants for preservation and research. Thanks to the Illinois Route 66 Heritage Project, created in 2001 to aid the development of the state's highway corridor, Route 66 in Illinois was declared a National Scenic Byway by the Federal Highway Administration. Challenges outnumber successes, but public interest in Route 66's history in Chicago provides a potential resource if community support materializes to preserve endangered structures in the city and nearby suburbs. By preserving Route 66, a traveler today and another tomorrow can explore the highway's legacy. For each who cares to look, the Route 66 journey begins again.

BIBLIOGRAPHY

Bird's-Eye Views and Guide to Chicago. Chicago: Rand, McNally and Company, 1893.

Brady, S. E. "Sixty Million Dollar Bond Issue." *Illinois Blue Book*. Springfield, IL: Office of the Secretary of State, 1917–1918: 67–73.

Chicago Numerical Street and Avenue Directory. Chicago: R. L. Polk Company, 1928–1929.

Clark, David G. *Exploring Route 66 in Chicagoland*. Chicago: Windy City Road Warrior.com Publishing, 2006.

Cook County Highways. Chicago: Cook County Department of Highways, July 1960.

Cronon, William. *Nature's Metropolis: Chicago and the Great West*. New York: W. W. Norton and Company, 1992.

Gorski, Patrick. "An Open Letter to the Members of the Federation from the Honorable Patrick Gorski, Mayor of McCook, Illinois." *Federation News*. Lake Arrowhead, CA: National Historic Route 66 Federation, Autumn 2002: 9.

Official Automobile Blue Book. Chicago: Automobile Blue Book Publishing Company, 1914.

Official Automobile Blue Book. Chicago: Automobile Blue Book Publishing Company, 1918.

Quaife, Milo M. *Chicago's Highways Old and New*. Chicago: D. F. Keller and Company, 1923.

Raklios, John. "How I Built A Restaurant Business." *American Restaurant*. Vol. 1, No. 3. Chicago: Patterson Publishing Company, December 1919.

Randall, Frank A. and John D. Randall. *History of the Development of Building Construction in Chicago*. 2nd ed. Chicago: University of Illinois Press, 1999.

Sheets, Frank T. *Highway of Tomorrow*. Chicago: Portland Cement Association, 1937.

Sinkevitch, Alice, ed. *AIA Guide to Chicago*. 2nd ed. Orlando, FL: Harcourt, Incorporated, 2004.

Young, David M. *The Iron Horse and the Windy City: How Railroads Shaped Chicago*. Dekalb, IL: Northern Illinois University Press, 2005.

———. *Chicago Transit: An Illustrated History*. Dekalb, IL: Northern Illinois University Press, 1998.

INDEX

ACROSS AMERICA, PEOPLE ARE DISCOVERING SOMETHING WONDERFUL. *THEIR HERITAGE.*

Arcadia Publishing is the leading local history publisher in the United States. With more than 3,000 titles in print and hundreds of new titles released every year, Arcadia has extensive specialized experience chronicling the history of communities and celebrating America's hidden stories, bringing to life the people, places, and events from the past. To discover the history of other communities across the nation, please visit:

www.arcadiapublishing.com

Customized search tools allow you to find regional history books about the town where you grew up, the cities where your friends and family live, the town where your parents met, or even that retirement spot you've been dreaming about.

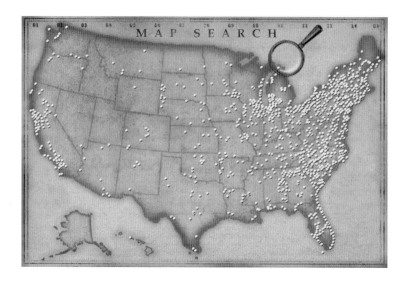